A Mom's Guide to Raising Pro-Life Kids

MAAIKE ROSENDAL & CHARMAINE VAN MAREN

Copyright © 2024
Canadian Centre for Bio-Ethical Reform

All rights reserved. No part of this book may be reproduced in any manner, stored in a retrieval system, or transmitted in any form or by any means without the prior permission from the publisher, except in the case of brief quotations in an article or review, subject to the provisions of Canadian copyright law.

ISBN: 978-1-998170-20-3

Published and distributed by Christian Heritage Press
www.christianheritagepress.ca

Interview requests or questions for the authors may be directed to email@endthekilling.ca

Cover design by Sharon Grisnich

To our children,

Thank you for teaching us how
to be pro-life moms

Contents

A Note to Readers 9
Chapter 1: The Case for Raising Pro-Life Kids 11
Chapter 2: God-Given Instincts & Words 27
Chapter 3: Talking About Abortion 45
Chapter 4: When Kids Become Teens 61
Chapter 5: Losing Children During Pregnancy ... 95
Chapter 6: Responding to Infertility 113
Chapter 7: To Be Christian Is To Be Pro-Life 133
Acknowledgments 149
Appendix 153
Endnotes 167

A Note to Readers

"What about us?"

"Do you have a resource for moms?"

"Is there anything I can do to make a difference while at home with my kids?"

We frequently receive these sorts of questions after pro-life presentations on behalf of the Canadian Centre for Bio-Ethical Reform, the organization we work for. These questions prompted us to look for such a resource—and, when we could not find one, inspired us to create one. Moms are perhaps the most significant force in the pro-life movement, and this book was written for them. Their requests led to the creation of *A Mom's Guide to Raising Pro-Life Kids*. We hope it's what you were looking for—and more!

What about dads? Fathers play a vital role in their families *and* the battle for our culture; thankfully, there are resources for them. However, mothers often set the tone in the home regarding life issues, and when there are two parents, mothers usually spend the most time with the children. This is why, as moms, we are writing to moms.

Finally, our book contains many personal stories, several of which are about our children. We have consistently written in first person for the text to flow better and, where applicable, to protect the privacy of our children. Combined, there are ten children in our families (at the time of publication). Without unnecessarily identifying them, we have shared some of their conversations with us about the issues covered in this book. We hope that this makes the content relatable to all mothers.

Happy reading!

Maaike Rosendal & Charmaine Van Maren
Tillsonburg, Ontario
Canada
October 2024

1

The Case for Raising Pro-Life Kids

It's late, you're tired, and you've finally tucked the kids into bed. It's been a long day; before you call it a night, you check your email. A friend has invited you to a fundraiser for a local pregnancy care center. It looks like an interesting event, so you make a mental note to check your calendar, and then log off and go to bed.

A few weeks later, your friend posts a picture of the event. You realize that it completely slipped your mind in the bustle of daily life. *Where does the time go?* The image is accompanied by a question: "If babies are dying, what will you do?"

The question lingers. *What should I do?* When babies are dying, obviously, Christians have a duty to respond. In college, you knew some people involved in the campus pro-life club. Your church helps local moms in need, and your friend's sister works with a political lobbying group, but none of these seem to be a good fit for a mom with young children. *Realistically,* you think, *what can I do?*

In the middle of meals, laundry, diapers, and school, it's hard to imagine also taking on the plight of pre-born children. You might even ask yourself, is that my responsibility right now? You've probably heard it before: The most pro-life thing you can do is to raise your children.

We want to make the case that this is true–with one addition: The most pro-life thing you can do is raise your children *pro-life*.

A biblical mandate for raising your kids pro-life

It is important to acknowledge that there are different seasons in life. Being the parent of a newborn is much different than being the parent of a teenager, and the parental role is dramatically different during these different stages. Every family has unique circumstances, but what we have in common is that we are the first line of defense in saving lives from abortion.

In Deuteronomy 6, directly after receiving the Ten Commandments, Moses instructs the people of Israel:

> And these words, which I command thee this day, shall be in thine heart: And thou shalt teach them diligently unto thy children, and shalt talk of them when thou sittest in thine house, and when thou walkest by the way, and when thou liest down, and when thou risest up (6-7).

With these words, we are shown what diligent instruction looks like: in our hearts, in the home, in the evening, in the morning, and while traveling. The command, "Thou shalt not kill," prohibits the murder of the innocent; therefore, these instructions also apply to teaching our children about life issues.

Each day, our choices speak volumes about what we truly value. Moses makes this clear when he exhorts the Israelites in Deuteronomy 30:

> I call heaven and earth to record this day against you, that I have set before you life and death, blessing and cursing: therefore choose life, that both thou and thy seed may live: that thou mayest love the Lord thy God, and that thou mayest obey his voice, and that thou mayest cleave unto him: for he is thy life, and the length of thy days (19-20a).

As pro-life moms, our parenting must reflect choosing life so that by God's grace, we and our children may live.

In contrast, the culture that our children grow up in is a culture of death. If that sounds too severe, consider that respect for many human lives is lacking. In a culture of death, society does not protect all human beings equally. Even worse, the weakest and most vulnerable are denied protection. The most obvious and horrific examples of this, of course, are abortion and euthanasia.

In his letter, *The Gospel of Life (Evangelium Vitae)*, Pope John Paul II writes,

> [It] is possible to speak in a certain sense of a war of the powerful against the weak: a life which would require greater acceptance, love and care is considered useless, or held to be an

intolerable burden, and is therefore rejected in one way or another. A person who, because of illness, handicap or, more simply, just by existing, compromises the well-being or life-style of those who are more favoured tends to be looked upon as an enemy to be resisted or eliminated.[i]

As much as we may try to shelter them, whether it be in Christian communities or at home, our children will inevitably face this reality. With a puzzled expression, one of my boys recently asked, "Why do people not like it when you have babies?" I tried to find out where he got this idea. "Everywhere," he responded. "When you're pregnant, people ask if it's your last one. And when you have a baby, they say, are you done now? As if it's a bad thing." Our culture generally does not view multiple babies as a gift. Our children absorb those messages sooner than we realize, even while coming along on something as simple as a grocery run. While *their* lives have been cherished from the beginning as a unique gift of God, the culture at large does not share this truth. Human life has become increasingly devalued from the youngest to the oldest.

It is our responsibility as parents to foster a culture of life in our families. It's the opposite of the culture of death: A culture that rejoices in life. Our children must sense our awe for the precious gift of life over which we are given stewardship. In our homes, we must have and teach reverence for life. What does this mean? Children must grow up being loved *and* taught that their lives—and those of everyone else—are of infinite worth. We must lay the foundation of life-affirming values so our children become grounded through years of a pro-life upbringing. Over time, we will teach them about the opposing views of the culture around us. But they need to grow up with a reverence for life while slowly gaining the tools and skills to defend the lives most at risk. When they face the culture that is so hostile to life, we pray that these will be the tethers that keep our children firmly attached to the pro-life worldview.

What happens when pro-life parents neglect this duty?

As with most moral issues, if children are not given a solid alternative, they will default to the cultural norm. There is no neutral ground. In the United States, they'll be pulled into the fierce culture war over whether abortion is acceptable. In Canada, mainstream culture constantly confirms that abortion is *good*. We may wish to believe that abortion is limited to the individuals who make that choice, perhaps as a "necessary evil." However, millions of people view abortion as a woman's right and even as completely ordinary healthcare. Pro-choice ideology is embedded into everything around us. If you think that is an exaggeration, consider the following.

Mainstream media in Canada and the United States consistently present abortion as being a woman's right, using terminology that hides the reality of what abortion is while dehumanizing the pre-born child. There's no shortage of examples of this. During the 2020 lockdowns, media outlets loudly supported the continuation of abortion as an *essential service* while countless people in actual emergencies struggled to access healthcare. While some media in the United States are pro-life, in Canada virtually none are. The main narrative is pro-abortion.

When those of us in the pro-life movement do media interviews, we have learned not to count on accurate or balanced reporting. Even the best interview gets spliced, edited, or cut out entirely to avoid a favorable representation of the pro-life side. Consumption of mainstream media will inevitably influence our thinking and the minds of our children. By what they exclude as much as what they include, by the stories that are covered, by the angle of the stories, and by their fundamental underlying assumption that abortion is a *human right* rather than a *human rights violation*, most media outlets tirelessly work at shaping our view of the world and insidiously erode our reverence for life.

It is this same media which informs the public about politics. In the political realm, one can scarcely mention going to church, much less being pro-life, without the media concluding that the politician is anti-woman and certainly anti-abortion. Those who stay silent on the issue, taking neither a pro-life nor a pro-choice side, are often hounded until they declare their allegiance to the abortion cause. To be seen as progressive or simply to avoid the scrutiny of the media, politicians parrot trendy buzzwords such as "reproductive rights" and "choice," never addressing what the choice is or what happens to the baby during the exercise of this "choice."

To get a sense of the messaging that the entertainment industry pushes, we went online and googled the phrase "celebrities and abortion rights." Within 0.34 seconds, over twenty-three million links popped up, outlining the support for, donations to, and personal testimonies of abortion by celebrities. The common theme? That "pregnancy termination" is considered normal, and that it is awful and archaic to oppose abortion.

The online publication *Teen Vogue*, which claims to cover style, politics, culture, and identity, has clearly taken up the torch for abortion rights. Hundreds of abortion-positive articles normalize and encourage youth to actively support the killing of pre-born children and skillfully promote it as a noble cause. Some provide information on how to obtain an abortion if you don't want to tell your parents. Several seek to normalize abortion by saying even staunch anti-abortion advocates sometimes get one. The message? "Don't worry, Christians do this too."

A story about pop singer and actress Selena Gomez was linked to this article. Many will recognize her name from her music and the child-friendly shows she participated in early in her career. However, in 2019 she was featured wearing a 1973 necklace, which is a symbol to honor the historic *Roe v. Wade* decision. The image linked to her

Instagram post read: "Stop telling women what to do with their bodies,"[ii] encouraging followers to volunteer for or donate to the pro-choice cause. Why this particular example? Her Instagram bio reads: "By grace, through faith." She's not a secular singer from whom we might expect the promotion of abortion. She's a self-proclaimed Christian, followed by teenage girls who might take their cues from a young woman like Selena.

Since the Dobbs decision of June 24, 2022, which overturned *Roe v. Wade*, the example mentioned above has proven to be the rule rather than the exception. Dozens of high-profile celebrities are using their platforms to normalize, promote, or even celebrate abortion, presenting it as a fundamental pursuit of justice.

This is also true for Taylor Swift, one of the most influential musicians of our time. For over a decade, the singer-songwriter avoided references to politics and religion, with dreams and love being the center of her earlier country-style music. However, in 2018, Swift stated publicly that she's a Christian in her critique of US Senator Marsha Blackburn. And yet, when the Supreme Court's decision ended constitutional protections for abortion, she posted on (then) Twitter: "I'm absolutely terrified that this is where we are–that after so many decades of people fighting for women's rights to their own bodies, today's decision has stripped us of that."[iii] Swift also re-tweeted a lengthy post by Michelle Obama, who shared her "heartbreak" about the overturn of *Roe v. Wade*.

Taylor Swift's view of abortion may mean nothing to us, but it wields massive influence on millions of fans worldwide. Having left true Christian values behind, she remains a powerful storyteller with the potential to shape the views of our teens.

The role of schools

As if that isn't enough pro-choice ideology imposed on our children, higher institutions of learning have also taken up the banner of reproductive rights. What happens when our children are not prepared? One of our friends attended a private Christian school and was raised by parents who consider themselves pro-life. Yet, when she attended a public university, she had no idea how to defend the views she grew up with. She began to research the abortion issue and became more convinced of and very articulate in defending the pro-life position. For many, however, a similar situation pulls them to the pro-choice side.

According to a 2024 Gallup poll on abortion, 40% of respondents without any college education identified as pro-choice, while 54% identified as pro-life (6% had no opinion). The poll outlines various levels of education, but in the category of postgraduates, the numbers are inverse: 64% pro-choice and 30% pro-life (5% had no opinion).[iv] In other words, the higher the level of education, the more likely one is to identify as pro-choice.

One significant factor contributing to this is liberal bias among educators. In 2022, an analysis of party affiliation of professors in seven American states (six of which were primarily Republican) found that all universities showed a strong Democratic bias among faculty.[v] When the professors were separated into Democrat and Republican groups, 92 percent identified as Democrats, and only 8 percent identified as Republicans. Social psychologist, researcher, and author Jonathan Haidt also found that professors are overwhelmingly liberal. Almost everyone teaching our children in college and university has a worldview wildly different from our own. Whether subtly or overtly, their ideologies create an environment that results in the abandonment of pro-life views.

We do not necessarily mean to discourage you from sending your children to further education. Instead, we want to highlight the importance of your role in preparing them for a time when they *will be* severely challenged in their beliefs.

Based on the many hours we've spent doing outreach outside of public high schools — engaging with students on abortion during their lunch break — it is crystal clear that public schools provide our children with an environment very similar to that of universities or colleges. Chastity is something most students have never considered, and abortion seems to be the norm. Our colleagues have talked to teenagers who have said they've had two abortions by age 15, many of them wishing they hadn't.

Additionally, public schools utilize radical sex-ed curriculum from a very young age, imposing a worldview entirely contrary to a biblical one. Among many other concerns, this prompted pastor and theology professor Dr. Voddie Baucham to assert, "We cannot continue to send our children to Caesar for their education and be surprised when they come home as Romans."[vi]

There are examples of Christian students who stay true to their beliefs throughout public school. However, much of the teaching you provide at home as a pro-life parent is proactively undone at school every day. Advocacy groups are well aware that to change the culture, they must target the youth, and they are doing so quite successfully. For the sake of your child, *consider this if he or she is in public school.*

In America, legislation surrounding parental consent for abortion varies per state. In Canada, no parental consent is necessary, and a school nurse or counselor has the authority to both recommend abortion and help a teenager obtain one. It should be a no-brainer, regardless of one's view on abortion, that this is circumventing the role of the parents and putting the health of the child at risk. As WeNeedALaw.ca puts it, "An adolescent who gets an abortion in secret is more likely to hide pain and complications following the procedure, putting her health at risk, and her parents will not know to watch for signs of physical or psychological struggling."[vii]

Education that does not flow from a Christian worldview will undoubtedly make the upbringing of our children in a hostile culture much more difficult. We're already swimming against the tide. We owe it to our children—and their children—to do the very best we can.

Christians have abortions, too

Our children are not only in danger of being influenced in their beliefs by a pro-abortion culture. Beliefs lead to actions. As hard as it may be for us to imagine, they are also at risk of having an abortion themselves. Looking at our family picture and seeing the smiles of our little ones, it's hard to believe any of them would ever make such a choice. Hopefully, they never will. However, we know too many girls and women from Christian, pro-life homes who *did* have abortions, and we'd be naive to think that could never happen to our children.

How is it possible that a Christian would choose abortion? From our experience, there are two main reasons.

First, some girls choose abortion because they *are never told what abortion is*. Their parents are pro-life, perhaps, but simply never thought to bring it up. Dr. Ziad Munson, in his book *The Making of Pro-Life Activists*, notes that most people who grow up in pro-life homes do not develop strong views about abortion because, as his research revealed, abortion is never talked about.[viii] As a result, Christian girls who find themselves pregnant may have never thought about abortion before their predicament, and they may have (subconsciously) absorbed the culture's messaging about unwanted pregnancies. Especially in a crisis, some may easily be influenced by a doctor, boyfriend, or peers, many of whom will say, very early in pregnancy,

"It's not a baby yet." Add to that the stigma attached to being pregnant outside of marriage, and a procedure that "simply" ends a pregnancy can seem like a good solution. One young woman close to us shared that she didn't have more abortions because she found out what it was *after she had her first one*.

Second, some choose abortion *despite* their pro-life upbringing. They know that abortion ends the life of a human who began to exist at fertilization but haven't internalized that truth or waver in the face of a difficult life situation. They may be pressured into believing that abortion is better or perhaps choose it themselves, knowing full well that abortion is wrong. We've been in conversations with girls who knew better, whose parents would have supported them, but who sadly went ahead with an abortion anyway. Those conversations are incredibly heartbreaking.

This brings us to an important point. We realize that providing children with a proper pro-life upbringing will not *guarantee* that they will not abandon this upbringing later. We are under no illusion that a specific type of parenting produces a specific type of child. The truth, however, is that kids *are far less likely to have an abortion* if they are raised pro-life in a very deliberate way. Yes, some children will still have abortions anyway, despite all of their parents' efforts. The same is true for drug abuse or other choices we fervently wish our children will never make. But when we do not purposefully teach our kids to be pro-life, we leave them defenseless in the face of our culture's lies — lies that, to someone in a crisis pregnancy, will seem very inviting.

Parents are essential to the pro-life movement because they can shape the minds of their children on an issue that can be a life-or-death situation. At stake are the choices and consciences of our children. If pro-life values are not passed on, the number of aborted babies in our country will also include our grandchildren.

Statistics back this up as well. In Canada, where there are no reporting requirements when it concerns abortion, we have no reliable data. In the United States, however, the Guttmacher Institute, which is Planned Parenthood's research arm, tracks abortion data and tells us that a total of 54% of women obtaining abortions identify as Protestant or Roman Catholic.[ix] In other words, Christians have abortions, too. Pro-life writer and activist Michael Spielman was spot-on when he said, "Eliminating abortion in the world begins with eliminating abortion in the church."[x]

How do we move forward?

It's easy to focus on the churches that haven't been steadfast advocates for life or the culture that aggressively seeks to recruit our children and youth. There's enough blame to go around, but pointing fingers doesn't solve anything, nor can we fix those problems ourselves. What we *can* do is make a difference in our own homes. The challenge for us, as parents, is to start (or continue) being intentional about raising our children pro-life. The good news is we're in the perfect position to do just that.

Have you ever had a moment where your son or daughter jumped towards you, completely confident that you would catch them? That is the faith your children have in you. Especially when they're little, there's no doubt in their mind that they can trust you wholeheartedly. They trust that what you teach them is truth. Unless they learn otherwise, they are designed to look to those who love them, especially their parents, as a trusted source of information. How often have we heard a child say: "My mom said…" or "My dad said…"?

Because of this, you have the ability to fill your child's heart and mind with small truths that hold tremendous value. Our children come ready to be shaped and molded by the parents they look to and trust. That may feel like a huge responsibility. It is also an incredible privilege.

The sooner we start expressing our thoughts about life made in the image of our Maker, the easier it will be for us to have these kinds of conversations, and the more normal it will be, both for our children and for us. Conversations are essential to creating a culture of life in our homes. If you've never had these conversations and your children are older: don't worry. If you're not sure where to start—hang on—we will provide examples in each chapter. These ideas can be put into practice gradually; before long, they will be second nature for everyone.

Parents, more than anyone else, shape their children in a unique way, especially at a young age. That's why you must be the primary source of this education. Moms, you have the power to make an enormous contribution towards the pro-life movement without even leaving your home.

2

God-Given Instincts & Words

We dropped by my husband's office for lunch when my daughter was almost two. As we chatted over coffee, she began to wander through the office, poking at this and that, exploring. She soon found a box of 11-12-week plastic fetal models and began to rescue them from storage.

"Baby! Baby!" she announced triumphantly, holding a fistful of the little models aloft, attempting to carry as many of them as possible. With that, she sat down and began to rock them, back and forth, back and forth. Noticing that my husband's arms were empty, she handed one to him, demanding he assist her in rocking the tiny babies to sleep.

As I watched them rock those "babies," it struck me that my husband and I had never taught her that these fetal models were replicas of pre-born babies. She had simply known, by looking at them and seeing a tiny head, tiny hands, and tiny feet, that these were babies. She could cradle them, protect them, and love them, just like she loved born babies.

As I think of this now, years later, another thought comes to mind: even the pronounced texture difference between a plastic fetal model and a living, breathing, warm, wailing baby wasn't enough for her to question what exactly she was cradling. Just by looking at them, she knew what they represented. We see over and over again that little children are instinctively pro-life. They know a baby when they see one. Babies are babies, and babies must be loved. It's that simple.

God is pro-life

It may seem obvious to most people reading this, but it is worth a sub-heading to state that God is pro-life, and therefore, it shouldn't surprise us that our children are inherently pro-life. The Bible is filled with explicit evidence that the Lord values human life. At many of our presentations, Psalm 139 is read, which is both fitting and powerful, as David expresses his awe of God's handiwork:

> For thou hast possessed my reins: thou hast covered me in my mother's womb. I will praise thee; for I am fearfully and wonderfully made: marvellous are thy works; and that my soul knoweth right well. My substance was not hid from thee, when I was made in secret, and curiously wrought in the lowest parts of the earth. Thine eyes did see my substance, yet being unperfect; and in thy book all my members were written, which in continuance were fashioned, when as yet there was none of them (13-16).

In addition, Samson, Isaiah, Jeremiah, Job, and

Paul all testify that the Lord already knew them in utero. In Luke 1, we read about John the Baptist, likely in the fetal stage, jumping in his mother's womb when his Savior, in the form of a human embryo, enters the house. It is abundantly clear that God views life in the womb no differently than life outside the womb.

We know that the entire Bible was authored by God. According to II Timothy 3:16-17, all the words of Scripture were "given by inspiration of God" or "God-breathed" into men to write down as the Holy Spirit led them. Therefore, the individual words are very important, especially in the original languages. When considering life and death issues, we should take our cues from the Hebrew and Greek words chosen to communicate God's thoughts to us.

In Genesis 25:22, Rebekah is pregnant with twin boys when "the children struggled together within her." The Hebrew word used in this passage for children is *ben*, which is also used for son, youth, and young throughout the Old Testament. In Genesis 22:6a, Abraham "took the wood of the burnt offering, and laid it upon Isaac his son." The Hebrew word used here for son is also *ben*.

In the New Testament, written in Greek, we encounter the word *brephos*, which means pre-born child, baby, or infant. Luke 1:41 refers to pre-born John the Baptist as "the babe [who] leaped in her womb." In Luke 2:12, the shepherds are told how to find the newborn Christ-child: "And this shall be a sign unto you; Ye shall find the babe wrapped in swaddling clothes, lying in a manger." In Luke 18:15, we read that "they brought unto him also infants, that he would touch them."

These passages, among others, show that God makes no distinction between children before or after birth. He chose the same words to describe both the born and pre-born because they are equally valuable in His sight. At the Creation Museum in Petersburg, Kentucky, the *Fearfully and Wonderfully Made* display highlights this, quoting Exodus 21:

> In the Mosaic law, the law of retribution is prescribed for a person who injures or kills an unborn child, showing that the unborn child is viewed with the same dignity and value as one who has been born (22-24).[1]

Since this is how the Lord views pre-born children, we ought to do the same.

We were created pro-life

Just as we must look in God's Word for how to

---

[1] Some Bible translations have mistranslated this passage, which then suggests that the perpetrator must only pay a fine if the baby dies, whereas "life for life" applies if the woman dies. As a result, this text is sometimes quoted to argue that the Bible values the pre-born less than the born. This argument is thoroughly examined and rebutted by Christian apologist Greg Koukl:
https://www.str.org/w/what-exodus-21-22-says-about-abortion.

raise our children, we should also look there for what the Lord teaches about life. The attitude about life derived from the Bible must be the attitude we adopt in raising our children. Since He is the Author, Creator, Sustainer, and Finisher of life (John 1:1-4), thankfully, He creates our children with life-affirming instincts as well. Though born into a broken world, younger children especially have a tenderness towards life. They are naturally in awe of creation and are drawn to what is vulnerable.

One day, one of our friends found a baby robin and gave it to my children to care for. They named the little bird Fleck after a character in one of their favorite books. For days, they diligently dug worms, feeding them to the little bird and even teaching it to peck at the ground to find food. The kids were starting to teach Fleck to fly when we sadly found it dead on the grass one evening. They were devastated. Their beloved bird received a proper burial, and they mourned the loss of his life for a long time after. While it's been several years, we still sometimes talk about Fleck and how sad everyone felt that he didn't grow up to be big like the beautiful robins at our bird feeder.

The Bible has numerous texts about God's care for His creatures, whether tiny insects crawling the earth, birds soaring in the skies, or cattle grazing the fields. He created them, and He cares for them. Yet, in the eyes of the Lord, we "are of more value than many sparrows" (Matt. 10:31). Children seem to understand the value of a human life, too. They instinctively care for a bird in need, but even more so, they want to love and protect a helpless baby.

We can't give our children these instincts; the Lord has already placed them in their hearts. We *can* nurture and reinforce what they were created knowing so that as our children grow up, this innate knowledge will have the deep roots needed to blossom and bear fruit.

Don't worry; you're halfway there

We hope you're feeling encouraged by the fact that you're not starting from scratch. We've been given a fantastic foundation from which to work. So, what does nurturing and reinforcement look like?

Our children, created in God's image, revel in the wonder of His creation. How many of us have asked our kids, "Who made the grass? The trees? The sky?" and they answered each question with: "God!" It's a simple yet profound way to connect with how they already marvel at what they observe in the natural world. What if we extend this to the wonder of life in the womb?

In Chapter 1, we mentioned the biblical charge from Deuteronomy, which was given to Hebrew parents and, by extension, all parents, including you and me. What is powerful about this model is that it involves teaching our children throughout the day, using teachable moments. Author Elizabeth George calls it "life-oriented, not information-oriented."[xi] Rather than sitting our children down for an information session, we speak truth into their lives during everyday activities and conversations. "We talk about what's important to us," she states. Isn't this also true when it comes to the pro-life part of our children's upbringing?

Imagine a child pretending to be a doctor or nurse bringing a stethoscope to you. After she listens to your heartbeat, you could say, "Guess what? Your heart started beating in mom's tummy when you were only three weeks old. How amazing is that?" When her feet have grown, and she needs new shoes, you may point to your pro-life baby feet pin and say, "Can you believe that when you were ten weeks old, your feet looked like this?" Or when she celebrates her birthday, you might give thanks for the number of years God has given her and include the nine months in the womb.

A pregnancy, whether our own or that of a friend or family member, is probably the most natural way to teach pro-life truths. During our pregnancies, we tend to talk a lot about our baby, sometimes in the form of "don't jump on the baby!" My daughter would lean over some days and kiss my belly, babbling about "baby." To children, there's obviously a baby–not merely a bunch of cells, nor an insignificant clump of tissue–inside that growing bump. All we have to do is affirm this.

Language is powerful

Pro-choice advocates have successfully used words to dehumanize the pre-born, for example, by calling them "products of conception." Even the terms embryo or fetus, though medically accurate, have resulted in viewing pre-born children as less or not fully human. As pro-life families, we can combat that with how we choose to refer to our children.

What if we refer to those yet to be born in the same way as those already born? When we intentionally humanize pre-born children and refer to them as persons who are merely younger than us, our children will follow our example.

When my husband and I wanted to tell our children about a new sibling, we took them out for apple fritters when I was seven weeks pregnant. When everyone had eaten theirs, one fritter was left on the tray. "Who gets the last one?" the kids asked. "I think it's for the baby," my husband joked. The expression on their faces changed from confusion to shock to excitement. "You have a baby?" one whispered incredulously. "Yes," I said, tearing up, "a tiny little baby." "We have a baby," they shouted with smiles and hugs. "We have a baby!"

Reflecting on this later, I registered that none of them said we were *going to* have a baby. They were just elated to have a new little brother or sister. After that, they told whoever they could. This caused both confusion and opportunities to share a pro-life message. "Really?" a store clerk said, for instance, "a boy or a girl?" "Oh, we don't know yet," my daughter answered. "The baby is ten weeks old now in my mom's tummy and has fingers and toes." The clerk's face cleared up. "Oh, your mom is pregnant." "Yes," my daughter said, "we have a new baby."

Humanizing the pre-born

We're not making the case that when pro-life parents say they're expecting a baby or going to have a baby, they're denying the humanity of their youngest child. It is not wrong to excitedly announce: "We're expecting a baby!" because the expectation of a child to be born is wonderful.

What we *are* saying is that, in a culture that denies the humanity of children in utero, we can intentionally use our language to say the opposite. We have the opportunity to combat pro-abortion influences by using life-affirming language to communicate this important truth: our lives begin at fertilization.

An example to illustrate: When I was pregnant with my second child, our family spent several months on the road doing pro-life work. This meant that our oldest child and I went out to eat regularly while my husband was giving presentations.

"How many?" the hostess would ask. "Two and a half?" (for I was visibly pregnant.) "Well, three, actually," I answered. "Right," she chuckled awkwardly. Situations like this don't bother me, but they show how the general culture doesn't view the pre-born as equal to us or even as fully human.

I also think of instances when people ask me while pregnant if I have another one "on the way." While we understand the intention of the question, in reality, a pre-born child is not "on the way" from anywhere. He or she is fully here, in the womb–the exact place a child should be for the first nine months of his or her life.

Ultrasound technology makes this very clear, allowing us to see the pre-born child with astounding detail. Pregnancy apps also include these images and are a fun way to involve born children. Our kids loved following the baby's development on the app from week to week and learned a lot about prenatal development along the way.

One of my early childhood memories was when my mom was expecting my younger sibling. At three years of age, my comprehension of pregnancy was limited, but I distinctly remember one day, my mother came into the room where I was playing and said: "If you put your hand here, you can feel the baby." That moment was my first time connecting pregnancy with a real, living baby. I'm grateful to my mom for sharing that experience with me, which highlighted the existence of my sibling while I was still so young.

With the incredible advancements in sonography and antenatal surgery techniques, now, more than ever, there is no denying the humanity of the pre-born. We can use this to our advantage. While my husband and I visited with pro-life sociologist Dr. Gabriele Kuby in Bavaria, Germany, she reflected on her own pregnancies:

> My husband and I didn't want to know the sex of our children–we wanted nature to keep her secret and wait until it was revealed in the incredible moment when the child emerges from the body of the mother into the light of the world. But, maybe now I would want to be told

the sex, because it allows a more personal communication with the pre-born to know whether I am speaking, feeling, and loving a boy or a girl. Whether I am touching and stroking and singing and speaking to an "unknown child" or to "my little girl" or "my little boy" — it would make such a difference to me.

Affirming parenthood from the start

As part of our organization's educational efforts, the team often does street outreach on sidewalks, outside high schools, and on college and university campuses. One of the questions that regularly comes up during conversations with young people is: "What if I'm not ready to be a parent?"

I recall talking with a university student who seemed increasingly convinced by the arguments I had shared yet hesitant to accept the pro-life position fully. I asked him if there was anything still holding him back. "Well," he admitted, "what if I'm just not ready to be a parent?"

"I think that's fair," I responded, "and I would encourage you to avoid becoming one. Based on what we've already discussed, the moment you get a girl pregnant, you *are* a parent. The question then is what you're going to do with your child and your parenthood?" He took a deep breath and replied, "Whoa, that's right. I'll have to think about that."

Time and again, we have to remind young people that sex is procreative and that parenthood begins at fertilization–because that is when a son or daughter comes into existence. To people who are already pro-life, this may not seem overly important because not calling ourselves a mom or dad during pregnancy doesn't endanger the lives of our own children. For many pre-born children, however, this knowledge can be the difference between life and death.

As we said earlier, language is powerful. What if we let our language reflect that parenthood begins not at birth but as soon as a child exists? Yes, our children are naturally pro-life, but they won't know the specifics unless we teach them. This will help root their God-given awe for life deep in their hearts so it won't be washed away when they encounter the forces of the culture of death.

Talking to kids about when life begins

While our children will recognize a 12-week fetus to be a human being, they, for obvious reasons, don't have the same realization when they look at a picture of a very young embryo. That means we should teach them that life begins at fertilization. If we don't, they will be told at some point in their lives that during early embryonic development, "it's not a human yet." If our children *know* (because they have been raised knowing) that their life began at fertilization, with the creation of an embryo, they will be far less likely to believe the lies our culture tells them.

You may have noticed our use of the word fertilization, where pro-lifers traditionally used the word conception. This is intentional, and we'd like to explain why:

> We often use the words conception and fertilization interchangeably. However, the word conception has changed slightly in meaning. To some, conception refers to the moment when implantation has occurred—the point at which the embryo has safely travelled down the fallopian tube and burrowed into the uterine wall, approximately nine days after fertilization has taken place. Terms are important here, because it is crucial that we are not misunderstood. Many believe that if an embryo is unable to implant in the uterus, a pregnancy never occurred. However, since life begins at fertilization, what happens in these cases is a very early miscarriage, the death of a tiny human being. While we are often not even aware of these tiny human beings, that does not negate the fact that they existed. Because no one confuses fertilization with implantation in the same way they confuse the terms conception and implantation, it is best that fertilization is the term we rely on in conversation.[xii]

Increasingly, good books are available to help parents teach children at various developmental levels about the beginning of life. These conversations don't have to be weird or include information about sex or human reproduction when children are very young. Also, each family approaches this topic differently, and that's okay. Some families may teach that life begins when a sperm fuses with an egg, whereas others may be more comfortable talking about a new life beginning when there is a tiny embryo. However, the more matter-of-fact we are as parents, the less awkward it will be for our children. They are naturally intrigued by and enjoy learning about where babies come from. We have included a list of resources that we have found helpful in teaching our own children about when human life begins.

Helpful resources

- *Where Do Babies Come From?* by Usborne
- *Wonderfully Made* by Danika Cooley
- *God Made Babies* by J. & L. Holcomb
- *Fearfully & Wonderfully Made* by Answers in Genesis
- *The Talk: 7 Lessons to Introduce Your Child to Biblical Sexuality* by Luke Gilkerson
- *Growing up God's Way (For Girls)* & *Growing up God's Way (For Boys)* by Dr. Chris Richards and Dr. Liz Jones

See also Luke and Trisha Gilkerson's website for articles and courses, including training videos for learning how to have these conversations: www.intoxicatedonlife.com/category/parenting/sex-ed.

Please use discretion and pre-read resources to ensure the content aligns with your beliefs and family culture.

When science points to God

Alexander Tsiaras, a mathematician and researcher who produces computerized scientific visualizations, created an incredible video of prenatal development from the moment of sperm-egg fusion. He commented,

> The magic of the mechanisms inside each genetic structure saying exactly where that nerve cell should go–the complexity of these, the mathematical models of how these things are indeed done are beyond human comprehension. Even though I am a mathematician, I look at this with marvel, of how do these instruction sets not make these mistakes as they build what is us? It's a mystery, it's magic, it's divinity.[xiii]

And isn't it? What if children learn from a young age that their lives began at fertilization? What if the facts about our first nine months are seen as fun, fascinating, and awe-inspiring ways to both marvel at God's creation *and* build a solid scientific base that affirms that we are human from the start?

When Alexander Tsiaras confesses that it is difficult not to attribute divinity to the nature of human development, he is very close to the truth. The complexity of human creation is infinitely greater than our minds could ever conceive, which is why it points to the One who created us. More than that, the development of children in utero is incredible because God makes them in His image, the *imago Dei*. Weaving biblical truth with scientific facts is a way of honoring His design.

Children are not inherently pro-choice

With all that has been written about children being inherently pro-life, it may seem redundant to state that kids are not inherently pro-choice. Their impulses and instincts are generally to nurture, protect, see, and recognize the humanity in other, smaller children. If we were to try to raise our children to be pro-choice, we would have to stamp that out.

This is why it is so important to raise our children pro-life from a young age. Henry Beecher, an American pastor and social reformer in the 19th century, observed, "It is not hard to make a child or a tree grow right if you train them when they are young, but to make them straighten out after you've allowed things to go wrong is not an easy matter."[xiv]

The more deeply rooted our children's values are, the harder the culture will have to fight for their minds and souls. If we implant these values into our little ones and spend the subsequent years of their childhood nurturing and reinforcing them, our children will be much better prepared to face a culture of death and able to reject its lies with confidence.

How do we know? Proverbs 22:6 reads: "Train up a child in the way he should go: and when he is old, he will not depart from it." Or, as the unknown author of the following poem expressed it:

Whatever you write on the heart of a child,
No water can wash away.
The sand may be shifted when billows are wild,
And the efforts of time may decay.

Some stories may perish, some songs be forgot;
But this graven record–time changes not.
Whatever you write on the heart of a child…
Will linger unchangeably there.[xv]

3

Talking About Abortion

When my daughter is tucked into bed at night, I sometimes run my fingers through her beautiful hair. On the top bunk, she's at eye level with me. During these golden moments, we mostly chit-chat about her day. However, some evenings are for more significant topics. "Mom," she asks this time, "why do some people kill babies?"

When we imagined parenthood, it is fair to say we never imagined talking to our children about abortion. Difficult conversations about sin and injustice don't typically enter idyllic dreams about raising rosy-cheeked boys and girls. But we live outside of Paradise, and sooner or later, we are faced with this reality.

We desire to protect our children

As parents, we naturally want to protect our children from harm. We may also instinctively want to prevent them from learning about scary, sad, or difficult topics. We wish for our children to grow up carefree and would like to avoid popping the beautiful bubble of childhood contentment. While watching our children chase butterflies, unburdened by the troubles that weigh down others, we've wished this innocence could last forever.

Reflecting upon this, our hearts go out to the millions of children who never had such a childhood or never will. It is an enormous privilege when ours do. It is not wrong to desire to keep our children from facing all that is wrong in the world. We must be careful, however, not to attempt to create a home environment that hides references to actual wrongs, such as abortion, for at least two reasons.

God sets the standard

If the Bible has a central place in your home, you have the perfect content and context for anything that needs to be discussed with your children. The creation account tells us the reason that each of us has infinite value: "And God said, Let us make man in our image, after our likeness" (Gen. 1:26). Genesis 3 explains the existence of sin in our hearts and our world, with many examples throughout the Holy Scriptures. The conception, birth, death, and resurrection of Christ provide hope for redemption, even after the killing of one's child, and eternity creates perspective for our life on earth. Each of these essential elements of Christianity, in a nutshell, touches on issues related to life and death.

The Word of God is often far more direct than we're comfortable with, especially concerning wrongdoing. While we may explain concepts in an age-appropriate way and only include the amount of information and detail our children can handle at their level of maturity, we would not do justice to the original if we left out the essence. We also miss the point if we do not apply these timeless truths to our own context. There are countless Bible passages and histories that are a good starting point for further exploration. Let's look at a few examples.

Directly after the Fall, we encounter Cain's jealousy towards Abel, which leads to man's blood being shed for the first time in human history. Cain must answer to God, who calls out, "What hast thou done? the voice of thy brother's blood crieth unto me from the ground" (Gen. 4:10). The gravity is all the greater because of the family relationship: your *brother's* blood. It is always wrong to intentionally kill an innocent person, but it is worse when he or she is someone we would naturally love.

Some might object that applying this to the issue of abortion goes too far. Some even make the case that the Scriptures are silent on abortion. This couldn't be farther from the truth. The Bible lays out clearly that it is wrong to kill innocent human beings: whoever harms a human, touches the image of God (e.g., Gen. 9:6)! The Bible does not need to mention every way in which one can be killed for us to know that it is wrong. We only need to determine whether the pre-born child in the womb is a human being. Both Scripture and science confirm this. We can conclude that, just like it is wrong to kill a child outside the womb, it is wrong to kill a child inside the womb.

There are Bible stories that help us explain this

to our children and bring up questions that help them apply these truths to their own lives. After one of my presentations, a woman asked how to introduce the topic of abortion to her children. Another woman raised her hand and shared that when she and her husband read about the slaughter of the Hebrew boys in Egypt, they felt this was a good time to introduce abortion. "Did you know that there are little boys and girls still being killed today?" they asked their children. Her advice to the other parents in the audience was to let these conversations happen naturally as we take our cues from God's Word.

In sermons about this history, multiple pastors have made the connection to abortion while pointing out that the midwives, unwilling to carry out the Pharaoh's orders to kill the babies, were blessed by God (Ex. 1:15-21). Reflecting upon this, we can ask our children to consider how we need to obey God more than man. We can also ask what *we* could do, very practically, to save the lives of those around us in danger of death.

There is truly no lack of Bible passages that can lead to conversations about abortion. Leviticus, Isaiah, and Jeremiah, to name a few, have strong words about the awful practice of child sacrifice. Is it any different when children are sacrificed in our nation? Proverbs 31:8 commands us to "Open thy mouth for the dumb in the cause of all such as are appointed to destruction." We might ask: who is appointed to destruction in our country? Do they have a voice? What does it mean to open our mouths for them? In the New Testament, the slaughter of the innocents in Bethlehem (Matt. 2:16-18) reminds us that the evils committed in the past are very much alive today. Though difficult, reading such histories to our children is an opportunity to ask: What is God saying to me? What does it mean for us? What is the significance in our culture?

That's not all. We must also share biblical examples of grace and mercy with our children. The most powerful one in this context is King Manasseh, who worshipped Molech. It is horrifying to read how he sacrificed his children by forcing them into the fire in the valley of Hinnom. In wrath, God allowed his kingdom to be overpowered, and the king was carried off in chains to Babylon. Yet, Manasseh turned to God in his affliction, repented of his sins, and was restored by a gracious God (II Chr. 33:10-20). When communicating the seriousness of abortion to our children, we should use histories like these to point to the redemption that is found in Christ.

This is not an exhaustive list of examples. Still, they demonstrate that if we read the Word of God with our families, it would take tremendous effort to exclude references to real sins–and the consequences that often follow–from the upbringing of our children. While parents could read the Word of God superficially, without drawing any lessons from Scripture for personal life, we know that the Bible is not just a history book but is meant to be a lamp unto our feet and a light upon our path. We ought to prayerfully let it light the way in our conversations about abortion, too.

The other side gets it

The first reason for not leaving the topic of abortion out of conversations with our children is that this goes against the standard the Bible sets. The second reason is that even if we don't address abortion with our children, those supporting and promoting abortion certainly will.

Curious about what is available online, we searched "how to talk to your kids about abortion." One of the first articles that popped up made the point: "If you don't talk to your kids about this stuff, you can be sure someone else will so make sure you talk to your kids."[xvi] Another article made the following case: "The foundations we lay when our children are young pave the way for the development of their ideologies, both good and harmful. Young people deserve factual information on abortion from people who've had them."[xvii] The sad irony is that both of these quotes are taken from abortion-supporting articles.

Pro-choice parents have to teach this view to normalize abortion and stamp out the pro-life instincts their children have. Many of these parents describe their children's initial confusion about abortion as a woman's right. However, with pro-choice instruction, they were soon advocates of abortion themselves.

Without the right framework, their inherent sense of justice is twisted to defend a choice that kills other children. It is both heartbreaking and infuriating to read accounts of moms justifying their past abortions to their born sons or daughters. Is it any wonder that to many teenagers, abortion is completely normal?

Perhaps there is one thing that we can learn from abortion-supporting parents: They talk with their kids about what concerns them. They're passionate about abortion, so they make sure it's something they pass on. In other words, if you deeply care about something, it is nearly impossible not to have conversations about it with your children. You might want to shelter your child from the truth of what abortion does, and that's understandable. However, when you live out pro-life values and feel burdened with the plight of pre-born children, the topic of abortion will likely come up earlier in your child's life than you expect, and you should be prepared.

What do you say?

We've seen why we need to talk about abortion with our children. The next step is to think about how. The topic will naturally come up in a Bible-centered family. But how do you explain what happens during a procedure that robs a tiny human of his or her life? What is too little or too much? How do you approach the topic in an age-appropriate way?

If we were to give you an overview of what is appropriate information for specific age categories, there would be children to whom those guidelines do not apply. That is why parents must take this responsibility of teaching upon themselves–because no one knows your child better than you. My sensitive six-year-old will likely process what we tell her differently from another six-year-old. In other words, proceed carefully and prayerfully while taking your cues from your kids.

For our little ones who ask questions about our pro-life work, we've explained, "Some people hurt babies, but we are working to stop that. We love you, and you are safe." That was enough for them. They nodded wisely and went back to playing. Questions often came later, when they had time to process it more. At the most unpredictable times they would follow up with, "Why do people hurt babies?" It is good to think about how you will respond to the questions that will follow the initial answers you give. "Because they don't believe that all babies are special," we might say, following with: "But they *are* special, aren't they? I've noticed you've been very gentle with your little brother (or doll or cousin, etc.)."

Depending on their personalities and level of development, older children will want to understand, often at the most unexpected moment. While snuggling our brand-new baby, my son looked up and said, "Why wouldn't you want this?" When we asked what he meant, he answered, "I don't understand why people choose abortion. Why wouldn't you want a little baby like this?" A difficult but important conversation ensued, which included two sides to that issue.

On the one hand, it's a good thing when we

don't understand how people can do something so wrong. Sin and evil exist, but when we can't wrap our heads around these realities, our conscience and instincts are thankfully in tune with what is right. We want to affirm this perception of evil and not try to explain it away while also helping our children understand that there are women who *do* want a baby but are lied to, pressured to abort, or who realize what they did when it was too late. We need to let our children know that the reasons a woman may choose abortion are varied and complicated but that it is a grace to see the evil of abortion so we can help other people come to know it, too.

Some kids, based on their personalities, accept at face value *that* abortion takes place, while others ask questions about why or how. We recommend that you don't share this information unless your child asks. How much will be shared is up to your discretion as a parent. You might introduce it by saying, "That's a difficult question, dear, but you know I will always be honest with you."

If you believe your child can't handle these details yet, you may respond similarly to how Corrie ten Boom's father replied when she asked a difficult question.

> Seated next to my father in the train compartment, I suddenly asked, "Father, what is sex sin?" He turned to look at me, as he always did when answering a question, but to my surprise he said nothing. At last he stood up, lifted his

traveling case off the floor and set it on the floor. "Will you carry it off the train, Corrie?" he said. I stood up and tugged at it. It was crammed with the watches and spare parts he had purchased that morning. "It's too heavy," I said. "Yes," he said, "and it would be a pretty poor father who would ask his little girl to carry such a load. It's the same way, Corrie, with knowledge. Some knowledge is too heavy for children. When you are older and stronger, you can bear it. For now you must trust me to carry it for you." I was satisfied. More than satisfied–wonderfully at peace. There were answers to this and all my hard questions–for now I was content to leave them in my father's keeping.[xviii]

When the time comes to tell your child, be gentle and attentive. "There are different kinds of abortions," you might say. "In many cases, a woman is given a pill that kills her baby. In other cases, the baby is sucked out of her womb, and that kills the child." In conversations with middle schoolers who've insisted on knowing how other abortions are carried out, we've explained that forceps are used to dismember the child piece-by-piece or that a needle with digoxin or potassium chloride is injected into the baby's heart, which kills him or her in-utero. Such horrifying information needs to be followed with a question to help our children process these awful realizations, such as, "How does that make you feel?", "What do you think about that?", "Would you like a hug?", or "Do you want to pray together?"

Kids need to feel safe

You may have noticed that, especially when our children are little, we reassure them of our love and their safety each time we talk about abortion. This is both intentional and essential. As adults, we can compartmentalize. Yes, abortion is terrible, but it does not threaten our right to life. Children, however, are less capable of such reasoning. I learned this from my son when he couldn't sleep one night and came down the stairs with a burning question: "Mom, can abortion doctors kill me too?"

When I held him reassuringly and told him emphatically they could not, his brown eyes searched mine. "How do you know?" he asked. My words felt awful and empty when I explained that the law dictates that only tiny children, those who are still in their mom's tummy, can be killed. I explained that that could never happen to him and that we would always do everything we could to keep him safe. He then asked about his newborn sister. "Because she's little." It dawned on me that he felt threatened by abortion because he didn't make the distinction between born and pre-born children like adults do. In other words, if someone can kill a tiny pre-born baby, what's stopping them from killing a slightly bigger baby, or even me?

It's heartbreaking to see our children trying to grapple with such injustice and insanity. Because they are instinctively pro-life, they know that no one should harm them, a baby, or anyone else. It is no wonder that learning about abortion and truly comprehending it can leave them feeling shaken.

Thus, when they learn about other children being unsafe, unwanted, and killed, we must ensure that our children feel safe, wanted, and loved.

Some time ago, our girls–born in the same year and best friends–were allowed to come along to the March for Life for the first time. To prepare them, we read *Pro-Life Kids* by Bethany Bomberger, an excellent book to introduce the abortion topic age-appropriately. We had explained that abortion supporters might be protesting the March and that they might be loud and angry, and they were. We had also prayed for the protestors. When the event ended, the girls approached several police officers and thanked them for protecting us. "It was a little bit scary," the oldest of the two said, "but as long as I held Daddy's hand, I felt safe."

When kids are upset

Letting our children know that we will protect them does not mean we prevent them from having an emotional response to the reality of abortion. Reassuring them that they are safe does not mean we tell them they don't need to be sad, which is an important distinction.

Perhaps you're afraid of the emotional response that the issue of abortion will have on your child. You may wonder how your son will feel or whether you will be able to comfort your daughter. You might even worry about how it will make *you* feel. What we have learned from observing children react to pro-life displays and presentations is that they are usually spot-on. What do we mean by that?

When given the facts about abortion, children almost always respond appropriately. They are sad. They feel upset. And they should feel this way.

When our children feel sad, we feel the urge to tell them, "It's okay." Except, when babies are being killed, it is most definitely *not* okay. Instead, we should validate their feelings. We can learn from our children when they express sadness or anger in response to abortion. We may have gotten used to abortion, but the reality remains the same. Helping children make sense of their emotions–by naming them, for example–is incredibly important. We should encourage our children to feel deeply for the children whose lives are ended by abortion and then follow their example.

While snuggling with one of my kids one evening, a little voice asked, "Is it almost done, Mom?" I didn't know what 'it' meant, but my heart sank when I asked for clarification. "Abortion. Is it almost done?" No mother wants her little boy or girl to lay awake, wondering when the killing of little boys and girls will stop. Yet, there we were. When tears trickled down my cheeks, I resisted the urge to wipe them away. *Learn from him,* I told myself. *When was the last time you lay awake thinking about abortion?*

"I hope so, sweetheart," I answered. "We're doing everything we can to make sure of that, and we pray for a blessing." "Can we pray right now?" he asked. *Mom and Dad are doing what they can,* he understood, *and we've brought it to the Lord in prayer.* Trustingly, he soon drifted off to sleep.

When children see abortion

An essential part of the educational work of our organization is showing both the humanity of the pre-born child *and* the inhumane nature of abortion. Similar to many social reform movements in the past, we display images of the injustice we seek to end. As a result, countless men and women have become pro-life, and many babies have been saved from becoming like the children in the pictures. When abortion is shown, abortion protests itself.

While we choose our locations carefully, it is unavoidable that, in seeking to reach abortion-vulnerable adults, we sometimes reach children. When children see abortion imagery, they instinctively know that something is not right. A little girl of about four or five years old once walked by our display, took one look at the image of a child aborted in the first trimester, and asked, "Who broke the baby?" Many other children have responded in a similar fashion, such as, "What happened to the baby?", "Why is there blood?" or "Look, someone hurt the baby." What is remarkable is that the child's parents' reaction always dictates the child's response.

Many pro-choice adults become angry at the sight of pro-life displays precisely because they don't know how to explain them to their children. The little girl mentioned above came with a man, presumably her father, who began to curse at our volunteers. He then turned to her and said forcefully, "This is what women get to do." She looked hurt and confused. Our hearts broke for them.

Sadly, this is not an isolated incident. Parents often become angry when their child's voice cuts straight to their conscience. Instead of facing the truth and acknowledging the injustice, they become mad at the pro-lifer who forced them to confront this issue in the first place. It is confusing for a child to realize their parent is more upset that abortion is shown than that abortion is done.

On the other hand, we've seen many pro-life parents respond calmly and wisely. A mother once kneeled beside her little girl, looked at our pictures, and said, "There are people who do this to babies in our country, but these people are trying to stop that. We will pray for them." Her daughter looked sad but reassured. Had her mom become hysterical, whether about the pictures or at the pro-lifers, her daughter would likely have done the same. Instead, this girl was blessed with a parent who guided her through learning about an awful truth in an age-appropriate manner.

That's our job. Let's resolve to do it well.

4

When Kids Become Teens

The year I turned fifteen, I often caught a ride to school with my best friend. These were the best days because we could discuss whatever interested us. It was also the year that Barack Obama ran for the U.S. presidency on a decidedly pro-abortion platform. I vividly remember where we were driving when she asked me, "What do you think about the pro-life and pro-choice debate?"

"I think I'm pro-choice," I responded. "I mean, it's a woman's body, isn't it?" She was shocked and exclaimed, "But that's killing a baby!" Now, it was my turn to be shocked, but at myself. I was against killing babies, born and pre-born, but, to be honest, I had never thought through the pro-choice narrative. I had never been questioned or challenged on these thoughts, either.

My friend doesn't have the foggiest recollection of this conversation, but it has always stood out in my mind as the moment when I realized what the "choice" in pro-choice does to pre-born children. I am deeply grateful that our relationship allowed her to call me out on this, for in that moment, I knew that I was pro-life, and I knew why.

Looking back, though I grew up in a Christian

home and was taught that abortion was wrong. somehow I hadn't made the connection that being pro-choice meant approving of or even advocating for abortion.

There are plenty of teens who, like me at that time, have not yet internalized the pro-life position despite their family disposition against abortion. How do we ensure that the values we carefully instill in childhood transfer to their teenage years? Or, perhaps you wonder, is it too late for me to teach these values since I missed the opportunity to do so when my children were little?

So far, there's only one teenager in our two families, so we don't speak from (much) experience. However, we have *been* teenagers. Additionally, our organization trains hundreds of teenagers yearly, and our teams talk to thousands of high schoolers during outreach. Along with talking to pro-life parents raising teenagers, those experiences have provided valuable insights.

It's not too late to start

What we've covered in previous chapters has been mainly geared towards younger children. Some of you reading this may be past this stage already, and while you'd love to go back in time to have those conversations, that's simply not an option. Has your window of opportunity closed? That question reminds us of a Chinese proverb: "The best time to plant a tree was 20 years ago. The second best time is now." In other words, start today.

Admittedly, there may be some bumps along the road as we and our children adapt to this new level of openness. Moreover, there may be some resistance, and that's not entirely unreasonable.

Having an honest conversation with your older children about this would be good. "We haven't talked about this topic before, but we realize now that it's important for you kids to know." This statement might be met with shrugs, sighs, or even eye rolls, but there might also be a level of interest. Don't despair; these conversations become easier the more often you have them. Your kids will soon recognize that this is something mom and dad care about, and hopefully, they'll start appreciating it, too.

While pro-life conversations with younger children can easily exclude references to intercourse, it is likely to come up when speaking with our older children. *How* to talk to your kids about sex is beyond the scope of this book, but if you're going to be open about pro-life issues, this conversation needs to happen. It's impossible to talk about the beginning of life and abortion without the science of how this all works. Further to this, it's challenging to discuss responsible sexual choices with our teenagers without a basic scientific understanding of reproduction. In other words, openness with teens about sexuality is critical.

You are the Information Desk

If you have already laid the foundation of a pro-life ethic in your home, you probably already work at Information. Your kids know that you are knowledgeable and hopefully have already gone to you with their questions as they've grown up. This is good. You've nurtured and reinforced values that respect life. The only thing left to do is to continue.

When children grow up, parents must be their safe, reliable source of information, rather than Google, social media, or their peers. There is no such thing as a stupid question. Whatever you do, don't laugh–more than anything, teens want us to take them seriously. When they confide in you, it is a sign that they trust you, and this is a privilege you should not take lightly.

This is not to say that you need to have all the answers; likely, you won't. Be honest about that. If you aren't ready to answer on the spot or in the moment, explain to your child that you'd like to think about it, pray about it, do some research, or discuss it with the other parent. (For those parenting without a spouse, a supportive friend or family member can be your sounding board.)

One mom shared with us that in such instances, it's important to follow up and let your child know when you'll answer their question. For example, "I don't have the answer right now, but I will find an answer by tomorrow night. Can we chat then?" We thought this was a great way to validate our children's questions and let them know we respect their trust in us by asking. It also guarantees an unawkward way to revisit or reopen the conversation.

If you are always ready to give or find an

answer to your teen's questions (and they *will* notice!), these conversations will progress more naturally and probably more smoothly. Moreover, once they know you're comfortable discussing life issues, your children will instinctively go to you for information.

> You might be surprised by, or terrified thinking of the questions your teenager could ask. Many teens have challenged us with thoughtful or witty questions during pro-life outreach outside of high schools. "Is it a baby before implantation?", "What do they do with the bodies of aborted babies?", "Is masturbation murder?", "What about back-alley abortions?", "Is abortion okay when the mother's life is in danger?" The book *STUCK: A Complete Guide to Answering Tough Questions about Abortion* by Justina Van Manen answers all of these questions and more and is a must-have for every pro-life family.
>
> "Let your speech be always with grace, seasoned with salt, that ye may know how ye ought to answer every man" (Col. 4:6).

Of course, you should also take the opportunity to initiate these conversations, informing your teens and even arming them against pro-abortion arguments before they come across them in the culture. If we do this faithfully, could it be that fewer young people will be confused or convinced by catchy slogans, faulty philosophical theories, and straight-up lies?

Recently, a mom asked us what to do if a teenager doesn't ask any questions or shows no interest in pro-life issues. Another mom shared advice based on personal experience and highlighted the importance of not forcing a conversation but regularly bringing up the topic, especially when the opportunity presents itself. For instance, if a Bible passage speaks of being known by God from the womb, we could comment on how amazing this is. Or, if women's rights come up, you might wonder out loud whether anyone considers the rights of the little women–the ones who aren't born yet.

Once we're on the lookout for them, it's easy to find opportunities to bring up pro-life ideas. When a mother in our church was placed on bed rest to prevent premature birth, we prayed for her and her pre-born child. We also gave thanks for everything that was being done to save the baby's life. At some point, I observed that children of almost the same age were aborted at the same hospital and wondered how that double standard of care made sense. With any of these conversation starters, we can leave room for a response without expecting one.

A more advanced example would be about the science of identical twins, perhaps because you saw them somewhere or heard of someone recently giving birth to them. "Isn't it amazing that one human being can split into two?" you might offer. "And did you know that people say an embryo is not a human until twinning can no longer occur?" Ask your child what he or she thinks of this idea, and explore it. I remember being stunned by this idea at university and doing my research afterward. I also remember the moment I read the flatworm analogy, which explains that each worm can be cut in half, after which there will be two living organisms. (The same is true for starfish.) It then raises the question: Does that mean there wasn't a flatworm beforehand? The answer, of course, is no. Similarly, the fact that one tiny human split into two at a specific time in human development does not mean there was no individual human being before twinning. Even if teens show no enthusiasm, you have offered valuable information that may come in handy one day.

The news cycle might also be an opportunity to invite conversation about life issues. Rarely does an election cycle pass without several heated debates about abortion. Discussions about euthanasia and assisted suicide (also referred to as MAiD or "Medical Aid in Dying") are ongoing as legislation continues to be pushed throughout the Western world. Make a mental note to bring this up at dinnertime, for example. If teens want to comment, they can. If not, they'll still receive the correct information about important topics.

When your teen wavers

What happens when your child becomes critical of the pro-life position and asks skeptical questions regarding your values? Many teenagers counter the statement that human life begins at fertilization with, "How could you say a one-celled embryo is a person?" Hearing that from your child can be hard. It would be easy, if not understandable, to respond in disbelief. But the response, "How can you say that after *everything* we've taught you?" likely won't engage your teen well, let alone win them over.

There are various reasons why teenagers begin to question the beliefs that we teach them. We must try to understand where they are coming from, which we can only do if we listen. Francis of Assisi wisely asked in his well-known prayer, "O divine Master, grant that I may not so much seek...to be understood as to understand." One way to gain understanding is to ask genuine questions to make them feel heard and taken seriously. A gentle "Tell me more" or "Why do you think that?" may give helpful insights into your teen's thinking.

Recently, I gave a pro-life teenager a ride to an event when, somewhat hesitatingly, he began to speak: "I am obviously against abortion–I understand that it's wrong–but I've been wondering about when someone is raped and gets pregnant. Would it still be wrong? I mean, does she have to have the baby?" I could have responded, "Of course it's wrong; it's always wrong to kill a baby!" However, I appreciated his willingness to voice this concern *and* his empathy for girls and women experiencing such trauma. Thankfully, I'd been trained how to respond well. "That's a really good question," I said, "and I'm glad you brought it up." He looked relieved, and I continued: "Sexual assault is a horrific injustice no one should have to endure. I don't know what it's like, but I do know that girls and women going through that deserve more support and that perpetrators should get harsher sentences." He nodded in agreement.

Then I asked, "If a guilty rapist doesn't even get the death sentence, why would we give the death sentence to an innocent child?" His eyes widened, and he replied, "I've never thought about it like that. That makes a lot of sense. But wouldn't it be hard to keep the baby?" We then spoke about women who, after having been violated themselves, chose to protect their babies by continuing their pregnancy: some parenting, others choosing adoption. I felt grateful for the opportunity to explore his questions about this difficult topic, hopefully solidifying his pro-life convictions.

Some teens may critique well-founded beliefs simply because somebody criticized *them*. We overheard a teenage boy debating with his father about human life in its early stages. His father engaged him in respectful dialogue, reiterating the pro-life position. They went back and forth a few times, and finally, the young man left the conversation with a "hmm." Later, in a group of young people, he defended the pro-life position precisely as his dad had. Though he had seemed critical, it became apparent that he was sorting things out in his mind to have an answer for his peers. He would have lost the opportunity to deepen his understanding if his dad had become defensive or angry.

Keep in mind that teenagers will still be going

through everyday teenage things. They may be dealing with hormonal changes, body image, or other issues that can influence their tone and mood. They may, however, *actually* be struggling with the pro-life position.

Why teens may struggle with the pro-life position

It could be that your teen is simply having difficulty grasping one or more aspects of pro-life apologetics. Perhaps they've come across a pro-choice argument that has stumped them.

I remember the first time I came across the concept of personhood and felt anxious about lacking a response to this type of philosophical argument. "It makes sense that human beings have human rights," I thought to myself, "but what about the pro-choice argument that says the pre-born aren't persons, and *that's* why abortion is okay? Is this where our position falls apart?" It was a tremendous relief to discover that much had been written about this topic and that there was, in fact, an answer.

More analytical teenagers may try to think through the pro-life worldview and run into trouble when they play this out in practical terms. Your teenager wouldn't be the first to be genuinely bothered by questions surrounding the ensoulment of embryos in the womb. After presentations, we have been asked, "If human life starts at fertilization, what about the many early miscarriages? Did those babies have souls? What will they look like when

Christ returns?" These are valid questions, and if not addressed, they will likely keep nagging at your child, possibly chipping away at their pro-life beliefs.

The truth is that there are answers we don't know. We should honestly express this, not as a convenient way to dismiss the topic, but to acknowledge that we deal with the same riddles. In conversations with teens, we've said that when we take the pro-life position seriously, we inevitably run into hard truths. How do we deal with those? Does it make us question everything we've believed so far? Or is it possible to maintain those beliefs, even without perfect answers?

There is much that we do not understand, at least not yet. For example, it is difficult to imagine what tiny children who died in the embryonic stage will look like when resurrected. However, we cannot base our beliefs or draw conclusions based on what we do not know. Instead, we should *work with what we know* and what Scripture reveals. Scientifically, we know that human life begins at fertilization. Biblically, we know that God creates each child as an image-bearer. Our limited human understanding and inability to comprehend all matters do not change that firm foundation of truth. Let's be honest with our teenagers and tell them we don't 'get' everything either. But the alternative–abandoning all truth–is far worse than not knowing all the answers. This way, we can model wisdom, reasoning, humility, and trust. One of our friends expressed it well when he said, "I can leave my finite questions in the capable hands of an infinite God."

Teenagers may struggle with the values you've taught because being pro-life is unpopular, often difficult, and definitely counter-cultural. It takes a tremendous commitment from teens to stay pro-life while immersed in mainstream culture. Teenagers may just want to fit in. While they care about babies having a chance at life, their pro-choice peers may portray them as horrible people who want to force a victim of sexual assault to carry her child to term. That's really hard. As parents, we must acknowledge that it's not easy to be publicly pro-life. Let's come alongside our teens, support them through this, and encourage them that doing what is right isn't always easy.

One of our friends commented: "My daughter insisted on doing a speech about abortion to her class. Her teacher had left it off the list of social issues to choose from. She told her teacher that was the topic she wanted to speak about, and her teacher agreed. She delivered a powerful, compelling speech. When she finished, her classmates were so hard on her that she ran to the bathroom to cry. While it didn't affect her steadfast pro-life position, it taught her just how hostile people can be towards the pro-life message. However, it enabled some other students to come forward and confide in her that they were also pro-life and that she was brave for doing what she did."

It is encouraging to find like-minded peers on issues we hold dear. Teens are more likely to be vocal and active in their pro-life convictions when they have an ally or friend. It's not always easy to find that person or pro-life community. It may require more effort from us as parents, for example, by attending a pro-life event with our kids or going out of our way to look for or create these opportunities.

What if my child is already pro-choice?

It would be heartbreaking as a Christian parent to hear our child say the words: "I'm pro-choice." No matter how much (or how little) time we've spent teaching the pro-life worldview, each of us desires our children to adopt the values we raised them with. We know these to be true, good, and beautiful–and to renounce them means abandoning a foundational part of Christianity.

If this is your situation, it is no longer about raising your child pro-life. As with a garden, in which you tend to young plants, watering and fertilizing them until they are strong and full-grown, so you also nurture and reinforce pro-life values. However, when your child identifies as pro-choice, as painful as that knowledge is, you are no longer tending to plants. Instead, it's about planting seeds again through respectful conversations about pro-life apologetics, combined with much love and prayer. Among others, books that may be helpful are *STUCK: A Complete Guide to Answering Tough Questions about Abortion* by Justina Van Manen and *Tactics: A Game Plan for Discussing Your Christian Convictions* by Gregory Koukl, who also wrote the following:

> When people say you can't argue anyone into the kingdom, they usually have an alternative approach in mind. They might be thinking that a genuine expression of love, kindness, and acceptance, coupled with a simple presentation of the gospel, is a more biblical approach. If you are tempted to think this way, let me say something that may shock you: You cannot love someone into the kingdom. It can't be done. In fact, the simple gospel itself is not even adequate to do that job. How do I know? Because many people who were treated with sacrificial love and kindness by Christians never surrendered to the Savior. Many who have heard a clear explanation of God's gift in Christ never put their trust in him. In each case, something was missing that, when present, always results in conversion. What's missing is that special work of the Father that Jesus referred to, drawing a lost soul into his arms. Of this work Jesus also said, ["Of all which He hath given me I should lose nothing, but should raise it up again at the last day"] (John 6:39). According to Jesus, then, two things are true.
>
> First, there is a particular work of God that is necessary to bring someone into the kingdom. Second, when present, this work cannot fail to accomplish its goal. Without the work of the Spirit, no argument—no matter how persuasive—will be effective. But neither will any act

of love nor any simple presentation of the gospel. Add the Spirit, though, and the equation changes dramatically. Here's the key principle: Without God's work, nothing else works; but with God's work, many things work. Under the influence of the Holy Spirit, love persuades. By the power of God, the gospel transforms. And with Jesus at work, arguments convince. God is happy to use each of these methods.[xix]

Let's talk about reproductive health

When I was in high school, there was a season where I suffered from chronic stomach pain. Exhausted and worn down, I went to my doctor to ask her to look into it more closely. My doctor had known me since I was a child, so she knew much about my family, background, and upbringing. Her nurse came into the office and asked: "Is it possible that you might be pregnant?" I was shocked: "Me? No! Not a chance."

She smiled at me sadly, as if I was a child with no knowledge about reproduction and she had a secret that I was about to be let in on. "It's okay," she said pityingly, "we don't have to tell your mom." I reiterated what I had said before, that there was no chance that I was pregnant, as I was not sexually active. She tried again. "Well, are you on the pill?"

Frustrated, I snapped at her. She made some notes and left the room. Some moments later, the doctor asked me again if there was any possibility that I could be pregnant and then sent me for bloodwork. I'd like to believe she took my word for it, but in hindsight, perhaps she had to confirm it for herself.

I am horrified retelling this as a parent. While it may be true that many, if not the majority, of teenagers are sexually active, the medical team pushed a narrative on me. It is appalling that the nurse implied that if I was pregnant, they could *take care of it* without my mother ever knowing. At school, the nurse had to call my mom for permission for me to take painkillers. Here, the nurse was suggesting that ending the life of a child could be done without any parental consent.

This experience is not an isolated incident. Everything in the culture proclaims to our teenagers that they can and should do whatever they want. Reproductive organs are for recreational purposes, and negative consequences can be dealt with later. Young people are encouraged or even expected to experiment sexually. It seems cruel that when sex has the result that God intended–the creation of a human being–support for the individual immediately wanes unless their choice is abortion.

Considering that this is our culture, it is nearly impossible to raise teenage girls without having at least one conversation about reproductive health. Still, many women we know were only given a book or had to find out from other girls if they wanted to know anything. Their parents undoubtedly did their best in the way they knew how. We recognize that much has changed in the decades since we were teens. As parents today, we face different scenarios than our parents. As a result, we must give our children the biblical view of sexuality at a younger age than many of our parents did.

It is encouraging that Christian parents are increasingly intentional about creating a culture of openness in their home, also concerning sexuality. Lest anyone misunderstand, this is not the abandonment of appropriateness and boundaries. Instead, these parents seek ways to honor God's creation, replacing shame with awe.

When the culture promotes the enjoyment of sex without boundaries, no one seems to mention the fallout, from heartbreak to sexually transmitted diseases to abortion to the breakdown of marriage. We ought to inform our children of these potential outcomes, as with any activity that carries a risk. But that's not all: we also owe it to them to speak about a better way.

Replacing the cultural narrative with a biblical narrative

Just as we marvel with our children at the wonder of God's creation in the womb, we may also marvel with them at the wonder of God's creation outside the womb. If we view our circulatory, nervous, or digestive systems as His perfect handiwork, why not also view our reproductive system this way?[2]

---

[2] We came across this idea in the work of Greta Eskridge, who speaks and writes about creating a healthy sexual culture in your home: www.gretaeskridge.com.

We are privileged to live in a highly advanced medical age. Now, more than ever, we have access to beautiful books on the human body, animated videos explaining our various bodily systems, and the ability to discover the intricacies of inner processes unknown to humanity not long ago.

What if we utilize this knowledge to communicate a sense of wonder about how their bodies are designed? This is especially important in conversations with pre-teens and teens as their bodies change. It is incredible, for instance, that a girl is born with all her eggs already in her ovaries and that (if all is well) her body knows how to ovulate each month. God created our bodies, both male and female, with a perfect plan. His plan also includes our reproductive system *and* a girl's first period. (How many of you remember it being referred to as "the curse" instead?) Teaching our boys and girls about this from a Christian perspective is informative, empowering, and gives credit to God as our Creator.

Teaching our daughters fertility awareness
We'd like to share an excerpt from a blog post titled, "I'm teaching fertility awareness to my girls. Here's why you should, too."[xx]

> *Fertility awareness breaks down fear*
> When we teach our girls to track their cycles, they know to do more than count numbers on a page. They can pinpoint the start of their period through cervical mucus and

basal temperature signs.

Fertility awareness alleviates confusion
Girls deserve to know what their discharge means. They need to know what is normal, why it changes, and what part of her cycle it signifies. Learning fertility awareness helps them interpret those signs.

Fertility awareness prevents degradation
Our daughters' bodies aren't flawed, and they don't need a pill to make it work right. Fertility awareness makes that evident, and encourages pride in their feminine characteristics.

Fertility awareness illuminates illness
When our daughters understand fertility awareness, they'll be more cognizant of warning signs for disorders and disease. They will know the warning signs of PCOS, and endometriosis; they can spot nutritional deficits and thyroid deficiencies. We can work together with our daughters to alleviate these issues, with holistic approaches that don't just triage, but treat.

Misconceptions [about] teaching fertility awareness

Now I realize I might be unusual, and there are those who disagree with me wholeheartedly. But the arguments against teaching fertility awareness to our daughters are unfounded, and we need to break through these misconceptions for our daughters' sake.

Misconception Number One: Fertility awareness is useless for young girls because their cycles are irregular

Incorrect. Cycle irregularity makes girls the perfect candidate for sympto-thermal tracking methods or Creighton[3] observations. As the poster child for irregular periods, this knowledge was a game changer for me.

Misconception Number Two: Teaching the elements of [Natural Family Planning] is overwhelming to young girls

Overwhelming, how? If we expect our tween daughters to learn Algebra, Biology, Theology, and the like, why are we assuming they can't handle knowing how their bodies work?

Misconception Number Three: Teaching the ele-

---

[3] "The [Creighton Model] relies upon the standardized observation and charting of biological markers that are essential to a woman's health and fertility. These 'biomarkers' tell the couple when they are naturally fertile and infertile, allowing the couple to use the system either to achieve or to avoid pregnancy. These biomarkers also telegraph abnormalities in a woman's health. The [Creighton Model] allows a woman to unravel the mysteries of the menstrual cycle." Creighton Model, "Creighton Model FertilityCare System," 2022, https://creightonmodel.com/.

> *ments of NFP is scandalous and too much information*
>
> What's scandalous about the beauty of God's creation? About the wonderful way a woman's body was made? There is much to be said for innocence, and society's working to strip it from our daughters faster than ever before. But do I believe that arming my daughters with knowledge of their bodies will abet in the destruction of that innocence? Absolutely not. If anything, I feel it will empower them, and open their eyes to the beauty of God's plan for creation. After all, why would you knock down a sand sculpture when you know how much detail went into its creation?

In contrast, mainstream society sees a functional reproductive system as something that needs fixing. In our post-Christian culture, we no longer function under the assumption that sexual intercourse is a gift from God to be enjoyed exclusively by a husband and wife. In previous generations, there may have been an understanding that sex was to be both unitive and procreative; today, sex is often seen as recreational.

As a result of the abandonment of God's design, our culture spends a lot of time trying to work around how He intended it. If our reproductive system functions as it should (i.e., monthly ovulation), or if sex results in fertilization (i.e., a child), something must be wrong. Since healthy fertility is treated as an illness, it is no wonder that hormonal birth control is routinely offered to women, starting at a young age. If abstinence is not an option, and children are not welcome, what else are you going to do?

Using hormonal birth control because of this perspective is, first and foremost, a foundational problem that cannot be resolved by talking about issues with the pill. Also, with our teens, we must go back to the basics. We should think about and discuss the purpose of our sexuality. If this is to bring glory to God, are we not held by His good boundaries within which we may use this gift? Should we not embrace the way He designed procreation to be the result of the two becoming one? Our thoughts and actions must be guided by a biblical narrative and guarded against the current cultural narrative.

Hormonal birth control

While functioning from a pro-life Christian view of sexuality and pregnancy, couples may prayerfully and thoughtfully conclude that they have a serious reason to avoid pregnancy for the time being. If this is you, and you're committed to being pro-life, do not ask your doctor for hormonal birth control. Often misinformed by medical providers, many pro-lifers are unaware that all options of hormonal birth control are abortifacient, meaning that they can cause an abortion early on, even before you know you are pregnant. Why not research hormonal birth control with your teen?[4]

The intrauterine device (IUD), for instance, prevents fertilization by keeping sperm from entering the fallopian tubes, which, by definition, is a contraceptive effect. The secondary effect of the IUD is to thin the lining of the uterus, which may prevent implantation. Thus, if fertilization occurs, a new embryo may be unable to implant. This is the abortifacient effect.

The Depo-Provera injection, the patch, the vaginal contraceptive ring, and oral contraceptives, commonly known as the pill, all work in the same way. They prevent ovulation (the release of an egg) so fertilization cannot occur, thicken cervical mucus to stop sperm from reaching an egg, and thin the uterine lining to prevent an embryo from implanting. Since women do get pregnant while on the pill, we know all three effects can fail. What happens if the first two hurdles are overcome but not the third? An egg is released, and a sperm fertilizes it, but the newly conceived child is unable to implant in the uterus, which causes his or her early death.

Perhaps you've asked your medical provider if this is the case, and they assured you that, no, hormonal birth control can't cause abortions. I've had such a conversation with my nurse practitioner and was genuinely confused about why she would state

---

[4] No resource was available to explain a pro-life view on hormonal birth control when we started writing this book. We highly recommend Justina Van Manen's comprehensive book, *A Pro-life Guide to Birth Control* (2025).

this. When we clarified our terms, however, it turned out that she didn't consider the embryo a child before implantation. It suddenly made sense to me. If whatever exists before implantation is "just a fertilized egg," then the thinning of the uterine lining is no big deal. No life is lost, and hormonal birth control is not an abortifacient. This is scientifically inaccurate. Sadly, each time an embryo can't implant in the lining of his or her mother's womb, a tiny human being loses their life.

This knowledge poses a simple but significant question to all pro-lifers: if using hormonal birth control can potentially cause the death of our very young children, perhaps even unbeknownst to us, can we in good conscience use it?

The morning-after pill

After pro-life presentations, teens frequently ask the following question: "What do you think about the morning-after pill?" The answer is always the same. "Good question, but what *I* think doesn't matter. What matters is what the morning-after pill *does*." We explain that since it is taken *after* sex, it may be too late to prevent ovulation or stop sperm from reaching the egg, which means there's only one thing left to do: thin the uterine lining. Then it's our turn to ask them a question: "Knowing that human life begins at fertilization, would it be okay to take a pill that could cause a child's death by preventing him or her from implanting in the womb?"

What's interesting is that teenagers often follow

this line of reasoning. "Hey, at least you're consistent," a young man commented once. "Inconvenient," another added, "but makes sense." Our teenagers should have this information as well. We can engage them by asking for their thoughts. It will allow them to form a well-rounded, well-informed opinion of hormonal birth control, which includes the (morning-after) pill. Hopefully, if a situation arises, this conviction will prevent them from being tempted towards hormonal birth control.

Abortion can become attractive

A young woman I spoke with said that the moment she realized she was pregnant, the following thought entered her mind: "If I have an abortion, nobody will have to know. It's not really a baby yet, is it?" Many others have admitted to thinking the same, despite being pro-life and knowing that life starts at fertilization. In other words, your pro-life teen wouldn't be the first to consider the morning-after pill or abortion when faced with an unexpected pregnancy.

The pro-life website Abort73.com includes a reference to the Guttmacher Institute, the research arm of Planned Parenthood. According to its data, 70% of aborting women in America identify themselves as Catholic or Protestant. From Abort73:

> Let that number sink in. Eliminating abortion in the world begins with eliminating abortion in

the church...Since pregnancy exposes the sin of pre-marital sex, abortion becomes a very attractive way for unmarried Christian teens to keep their sin under wraps.[xxi]

This is not new to modern times. In Old Testament times, King David sought to cover up his sin by killing Uriah after sinning against him, Bathsheba, and God. It solved his problem in the short term, although it dishonored God, and the consequences were devastating.

Similarly, in a crisis, and without repentance, abortion can seem like the way out. At least in the short term, it will solve an enormous problem–and enough voices are eager to tell teens just that. Does anyone mention that their relationship with God and their pre-born child will pay the price?

If a teen isn't sure how a pregnancy announcement will be received at home, abortion will be all the more attractive. But what if teens know that their home is a place of unconditional love and support to turn to, especially when in trouble? Could it be that they'll reject abortion in their own lives or bring a pregnant friend home because mom or dad will be there, no matter what?

The best way for our children to know how we will react to an unplanned pregnancy is by how we've talked about it or responded to others facing it. Suppose kids know from childhood that their parents don't judge others but show compassion, regardless of the reason for people's difficult situations. If that is the case, they may be more likely to open up about their pregnancy.

Pro-life families must come to terms with the fact that, in many ways, our teens may be even more vulnerable to abortion than their peers. They may worry about what a teen pregnancy may do to your reputation or the family name. They may want to avoid being a poster child for the pregnant teen they've so often heard about in presentations.

"I love you."

Someone who can speak about this from experience is Bryan Kemper, pro-life activist and youth director for Priests for Life. In a powerful article entitled "How Do You Answer Your Teenage Daughter When She Tells You She's Pregnant?"[xxii] Bryan writes:

> I can honestly say that when they were young I never imagined that one of my own daughters would be that scared teenage girl who is terrified of telling her parents she's pregnant. I just assumed that they would grow up, fall in love, get married and then have kids.
>
> The day I walked into the hallway and saw my precious [daughter] crying and afraid to tell me what I already knew was a difficult day. Not because I had to face the reality that my daughter is pregnant but because I had to see that fear in her eyes and hear her say the words, "Are you mad at me, Dad?"

To be honest, anger was the last emotion I felt at that moment. I hugged my daughter tight and just told her I loved her.

Bryan says the first words out of a parent's mouth when their teen shares news of their pregnancy should be "I love you." Unfortunately, this is not always the case:

> Over the years, I have talked to many kids from Christian homes, pastor's daughters and even pastors themselves who were walking into abortion mills because they were afraid of how people would react. I have heard pastors talk about how they feared what their church members would say [after finding] out their child got pregnant out of wedlock. I have heard young girls tell me they were afraid if their parents found out that they would be kicked out of the house and disowned. An angry father once threw me to the ground as he pushed his crying daughter into the abortion mill to make her have an abortion she didn't want.
>
> I am going to say something that may not sit well with many people: the abortion rate in churches is directly caused by those who forget the mercy and grace Christ shows us on a daily basis. It blows my mind that we would be more worried about hiding a sexual sin than accepting the gift of life. Instead of embracing the absolute grace of God we reject life itself and destroy His image.

Pregnancy is not a sin; pregnancy is not a disease, and pregnancy is not something to ever be ashamed of. Every single child is a blessing from the Lord and should be welcomed and embraced with all the love in the world.

Bryan Kemper is right: children are a blessing. While extramarital sex is a sin, a child is not. While the wages of sin are death, a new life is being knitted in the womb. It's humbling and beautiful to consider that the consequence of sin can be a child, a gift from God, as a token of His goodness for undeserving sinners. And isn't that what we all need?

Fostering pro-life friendships

Perhaps your kids are still young, like ours are, and teen pregnancies seem to be a world away from yours. Perhaps your kids are already teens, but you haven't faced such a difficult situation. Regardless, each of our children will need something important: pro-life friends. Peers become increasingly influential as kids grow up, so it would be wise for us to focus some attention here.

When our children are little, we can foster their friendships more easily by choosing playdates and guiding their time with other kids. As they get older, this is far more challenging. We've talked with friends who are navigating this aspect of having teens. We see them doing many things well, which we hope we can implement in our families.

- **Be genuinely interested** in your teen, even if their interests differ from yours.
- **Engage in activities together**, such as sports, games, and nature walks. Good conversations often happen when driving to and from places.
- **Delay owning a smartphone** as long as possible, or not at all. If your teen has one, **have ongoing conversations** about using technology wisely while modeling this as parents.
- **Create a home where teens feel welcome** to drop in, chat, join for dinner, or just hang out on the couch.
- **Maintain friendships** with families that have the same values
- **Encourage pro-life activism and invite others along**: this may include your annual March for Life, educational evenings, a local Crash Course in pro-life apologetics, dinners, etc.

Changing the narrative

Sometimes, it may seem that the only way to look forward to the teen years is with a healthy dose of apprehension. More than once, the well-meant advice of parents with older kids has been to "enjoy them while they're still small!" Surely, we've all heard the saying, "Little kids, little problems; big kids, big problems." Undoubtedly, parenting can become more difficult as the issues our children face become more complicated. But what if we change the narrative?

Some may chuckle and say, "Easy for you to say; you haven't gone through (much of) it," and you're right. We've only just started. That's why we appreciated the perspective of Greta Eskridge, author of *Adventuring Together: How to Create Connections and Make Lasting Memories with Your Kids*, but also mother to teens and young adults. She described deciding one day that a negative narrative was *not* going to be her family's story. She frequently encourages parents to find joy in the teenage years:

> Here's the thing about teens and almost teens: they are so much fun to be with!
>
> I think I love being with my kids now more than I ever have before. They make me laugh all the time. We joke together, tease each other and act silly together. They also ask great questions and have deep thoughts. We have incredible conversations about all kinds of things. They are interesting people.
>
> They put up with my happy freakouts when I see a rainbow, a teeny frog or a gorgeous sunset. They don't roll their eyes too much when I'm giving them yet another talk about the harmful effects of porn. They stop and pray with me when I tell them someone needs prayer. Or I do.
>
> We are friends. Whoever said you shouldn't be friends with your kids was really missing out.

Of course I'm still the mom. Trust me, they know when I pull the mom card. But that doesn't mean we don't also deeply enjoy each other's company. As friends do.

And, yes, there are also a couple days every month when their exuberant presence...... overwhelms me. That's when I say, "guys, my hormones can't handle you right now. I'm going to my room." They get it, 'cause they're hormonal too. And we have all learned to give each other space and grace in the hormonal moments.

I think teens are a lot like toddlers. They have big emotions and are trying to figure out the world. Sometimes it's just overwhelming. In those moments they can be challenging. But they're also full of so much joy! Toddlers are some of the most joyful creatures I know. Teens can be too. I like mine a lot.[xxiii]

We don't want to underestimate the many challenges of raising teenagers, especially in the culture we are living in today. The world is attractive. We also don't want to imply that if a teen struggles or makes poor decisions, it must result from poor parenting. Much of one's identity forms during adolescence, so bumps in the road are normal. Raising a teenager is hard, but being a teenager is hard, too. Perhaps even more than in earlier years, teens need parents who are open and prayerful, engaged and dependable. The examples of friends and acquaintances raising teens in this way, even during difficult times, demonstrate that walking alongside children on their way to adulthood is both possible and a privilege. And they inspire us to be hopeful.

5

Losing Children During Pregnancy

It is impossible to talk about life in the womb without recognizing the pain linked to this topic, whether from losing children during pregnancy or from facing infertility. As mothers, we must know how to approach these matters with sensitivity and compassion because our words and actions–also relating to loss and grief–send powerful messages to our children. Since each human life is a gift from God, our response to the loss of such a life will be guided by that truth. We risk undermining the pro-life values that we teach our children in good times if we don't model a pro-life response in hard times.

While we've walked with others enduring such pain, we have not experienced it ourselves. We could have written about these topics from a theoretical perspective, but we wished to learn from women who personally walked this difficult road. We wanted their voices to guide us through the sensitive and complex nature of losing children during pregnancy. We are very grateful to the many women willing to speak with us. To honor their privacy, we use pseudonyms.

This chapter addresses losing children during pregnancy, and the following chapter addresses infertility. Much of the information we received won't fit into this book, yet it helped us better understand a road we haven't walked. Thank you to all those who opened up about a deeply personal part of your lives. We could not have written these chapters alone, and we hope that your stories will create a greater understanding of how life, loss, and love are impossible to separate in a pro-life worldview.

Losing a little one

When one of our friends experienced a miscarriage, I had the privilege of seeing her baby. While the sex couldn't yet be confirmed, our friend thought of him as a boy and gave him a beautiful name. He was a little bigger than an inch. We could see his minuscule hands and feet, the fingers and toes still webbed. His heart had already been beating for more than a month, and brainwaves may have been present before his passing. Perfectly formed, he was now perfectly still.

Coming face to face with this tiny person was profoundly moving. There was no question about it: while only about two months old, this was a baby, and our friend had just lost her child. She grieved losing him. She still does.

All the stories we received from women who lost a child during pregnancy deeply expressed the lasting pain and empty places in their hearts. Jessica, who has lost two children during pregnancy, wrote: "It gets better with time, but you are still going to be hit hard with it sometimes. The hard days get further and further apart, but you will always miss your baby."

Why would this come as a surprise? Would any of us ever forget our born children? Could it be, however, that even as pro-lifers, we don't always value pre-born children in the same way that we value born children? Pro-life professor and friend Dr. Jacqueline Abernathy pointed out the inconsistency, having experienced miscarriages herself:

> We would never tell parents who have lost an infant that "it happens," and they can have another baby–because we recognize the baby [was] a unique human life. But that baby and his/her uniqueness did not manifest upon contractions. That baby was the person he/she became at conception. Pro-lifers supposedly know this but still suggest to me that another baby will even things out and all will be well. As if a widow can remarry and never mourn their first spouse. Since spouses are human they are not interchangeable. Neither are children *at any age*. Adding to the family through marriage or additional children will certainly bring new joy. But it won't be an even trade. We miss the unique humanness of those in our family who died and always will.[xxiv]

Several of the women confirmed the discrepancy between the values of people who are pro-life and the way they responded to their loss. Jessica shared the following:

Some people (even those who strongly believe that a pre-born baby is a person) don't understand how you can grieve the loss of a person you never met. And they will say so. They expect that you can just move on and forget what happened. They will say things like "You will have more children," or "God needed them in heaven more than you needed them here," and other insensitive things. Others will say that the baby you have after a loss (sometimes called a rainbow baby because of the healing and hope this baby often brings) takes the place of the baby you lost. No, it doesn't! They are both unique people, and nothing can ever replace the baby that was lost via miscarriage or stillbirth. We need to *think* about what we say and be consistent.

Reading through the experiences of many women, we especially noticed that last phrase. Many insensitive comments are likely made from a genuine desire to make someone feel better. However, as pro-lifers, we need to think about what we say and be consistent. This is as true when talking with pro-choice people about the humanity of pre-born children as when speaking with fellow pro-lifers about the lost lives of their little ones. And it is equally important to model sensitivity and consistency to our children.

Comparing losses

In conversations about miscarriage and stillbirth, the word "only" often surfaces in an attempt to minimize one pain in comparison to another. Samantha explained that, though she felt that her baby was recognized as a child, her loss was "kind of brushed off as a lesser loss when another family member had a stillborn."

Some respond that every loss is equal. Hannah suggests that we seek a more balanced approach by saying that various losses "are different for sure and need to be treated differently, not less, just different."

Instead of comparing and contrasting, it would be better to recognize that every loss is unique and, as such, validate the grief of each parent in their situation. Blogger Jenny Albers suggests that, rather than remind parents of what others had to go through, we focus on what–and who–was already there:

> I don't know the details of anyone else's loss, nor can I say I know exactly how they were affected by loss. But I do know that there is no "only" in pregnancy loss. Not in mine or anyone else's. There is "already." There was a pregnancy that had already progressed to six, or eight, or twenty weeks along. There was already life, as evidenced by two pink lines. The same pink lines that had already alerted a woman to her role as mother. There was already the sound of a heartbeat, whether it beat for a day, a month, or longer. There was already a connection between mother and baby. And there was

already love planted deeply in a mother's heart. A love that had already begun to grow from the moment the first sign of life was displayed in the once-empty window of a pregnancy test. It doesn't matter if a pregnancy "only" lasted for a few weeks. It doesn't matter if it was an early loss or a late loss. What matters is that there was already a baby who was loved immensely. And love cannot be measured in weeks.[xxv]

It is love that makes the loss hurt so much. It is also love that compels us to support the hurting.

Support from the community

Women mentioned that their community's response to their anguish, while often helpful, could, at times, be harmful. We can learn from these examples to live up to a better standard and avoid making the same mistakes.

Rachel messaged me about her four miscarriages. She has seen both the good and the bad when it concerns responding to someone losing their child during pregnancy. After her first miscarriage, she received "no support, no [one] grieving with me, but I was signed up for the church nursery without asking." Thankfully, close friends and family supported her and her husband well. After her third miscarriage, however, her new church community donated and served the funeral lunch:

> So many people sent cards and told us how they were praying for us. I especially appreciated the

specific Bible verses that people would share. They'd say, "I was reading my devotions this morning, and came across this verse and thought of you." Even a Kleenex passed down the pew–it's the little things that say, *I see you, and I care. Your pain matters.*

Jessica confirms this:

Our church is exceptionally amazing, but because we were so open about our losses and let ourselves be vulnerable, others were able to be vulnerable, too. Couples who had lost little ones 20, 30, or 40 years ago told us about the [children] they had lost. They hugged us, cried with us, and gave us meals.

Many of the women expressed that they felt validated in their loss. This is crucial if we are serious about our pro-life convictions and care about the people around us. If each pre-born child has infinite value, wouldn't our response to the end of his or her life on earth show this? By practically supporting fellow parents, not only do we affirm the value of their baby and the validity of their grief over losing their child, but we also model to our children what it means to be pro-life in word and deed.

How can we help?

Our response to the death of very young children–because that's what miscarriage and stillbirth are–speaks volumes about their value and the way we view them. The last thing we want to model to our children is that the lives of pre-born children who pass away don't matter or matter less. That doesn't necessarily mean we know what to say or how to react.

Most of us *don't* know. Even those who have navigated this before don't claim that their experience means they know what is needed in those difficult moments.

What we do know is that we should never use the phrase "at least..." Many women expressed dismay at being told "at least" in an attempt to cheer them up. Sophia writes:

> There is no *at least* when a child has been lost. No matter when, how old, or how long we were aware of a baby's existence, the loss of him or her is a tragedy—a tiny, unique individual has been lost. When someone shares that they have lost a child at any age or stage, never try to make them feel better by telling them about your cousin who has cancer or the homeless person you saw by the side of the road. Countless tragedies are happening all around the world: acknowledging the difficulty another is living through does not belittle these tragedies, and it certainly does not make someone feel better. To a certain degree, we are not supposed to feel better. In a sense, I was relieved that I struggled so much with the loss of our babies—they deserved our pain and our tears.

> Things to avoid saying to someone who has experienced loss during pregnancy:
> - "It's just like a heavy period, right?"
> - "At least…"
> - "It was still early."
> - "Don't worry, you're young."
> - "It just wasn't meant to be."
> - "You can try again soon."
> - "Sometimes God takes a baby because it would not have survived anyway."
> - "Good thing you will/already have others."
> - "Maybe it's just not meant for you."
> - "It wasn't even a real baby yet."
> - "Isn't it time for you to move on?"

Rose, who lost her son during pregnancy, writes,

> Our friends did everything in their power to help us go through our grief despite not knowing how. "We were so shocked, we didn't know what to do," they would say. "We did so much googling before meeting up with you. We don't know what to say. We can't even imagine what you're going through right now." They were right. We were so grateful for their efforts but we also felt so alone. *Why doesn't anyone talk about this,* I thought. *If it's so common, why do we feel we're going through this alone?*

Amber, having experienced two miscarriages, shared a similar experience. "Most people were sympathetic for a short time, but my grief was not so short-lived, and for several months I felt an utter loneliness from all support people, even my husband." She pleads for grace and compassion "even" after early losses. "Those who haven't experienced it can also help by showing compassion and grace to others for as long as the grieving ones need it. Which is always longer than you think it is when judging by appearances."

That is good advice. Morgan, who lost her little boy at nine weeks, wrote, "It is really almost impossible to understand the sorrow of being a mother without a child unless you are also a mother without a child." This is why Amber suggests simply telling your friend, "I don't know what to say. How can I help you? What can I do for you? How can I support you through this?" Other moms have suggested making a meal or sending a card, as we would do when a born child dies. This allows us to come alongside friends and gives our children an example of how they can respond when a little one loses his or her life. Most importantly, it validates the child's life, no matter how short. This is at the heart of being pro-life and raising our children pro-life.

When my friend lost her little one during pregnancy, her husband shared the sad news with us just days after they had announced their pregnancy. I explained to my children that our friends had lost a baby. Of their own initiative, the kids made cards and drew pictures, adding expressions of sympathy, such as, "Praying for you" and "I'm so sorry to hear that your baby died." When we asked our friends how we could help, they said they had received meals, but a hug would be nice. "We're just not up for visiting right now." Later, they shared that the flowers and cards we dropped off were a ray of sunshine during very dark days but that they especially appreciated the way it honored the life of their little one. As a family, we were grateful that by being direct with us, they allowed us to serve them in a helpful way. It was incredibly meaningful for our children to be included in their grief, and we hope they'll take this with them as they grow up.

What do you tell your children?

During swimming lessons, my children were chatting with other swimmers when I heard a little girl say, "There are four kids in my family: my two brothers, me, and the baby that died." "Oh!" another child responded, "When did it die?" "Before I was even born," she replied, matter of factly, "but my mom says the baby will always be part of our family." She included her older sibling because her mom does. His legacy lives on, not only in her parents' hearts but also in the lives of the rest of his family.

If the mothers who shared their experiences with us had other children, we asked them what they told them about the death of their child. Amber responded, "I didn't explain the loss to either [of them] at the time, but as they've grown up, we have definitely had discussions about when babies die in their mommy's belly and that we have lost two of our babies this way."

Sometimes, we may be tempted not to tell children, or others, about pregnancy early on for fear of miscarriage and having to tell them about the end of that child's life. Since we do not know the pain of losing a child during pregnancy, we also do not know what it is like to hold our breath during a subsequent pregnancy, hardly daring to hope that this time the baby will survive. Mothers who've had multiple losses explained they were too afraid to celebrate a new pregnancy by sharing it with their family and friends. However, waiting with the announcement also took away much of their joy about the latest addition to their family.

Hayley wrote, "That people can't reveal their pregnancy until after 13 weeks because of risk of losing the baby assigns a sense of shame [about] the loss–that it shouldn't be talked about or mentioned to others–when it does happen." In other words, if you don't tell anyone, does that make your grief less valid or authentic? Did the baby not exist?

Dr. Abernathy urges that "a child that follows the death of their sibling has every right to be delighted in just like their sibling was and parents have every right to rejoice in their baby, especially following a heartbreak."[xxvi]

Stephanie Gray Connors, in her article "Living with LaeLae: Thoughts on my Miscarriage," expresses the same sentiment:

One very supportive friend gently suggested that if my husband and I get pregnant again, we might consider waiting a little longer before telling people. My friend meant well, but I have a different view. People are unique, and life experience and personality are contributing factors to how we respond to things, but cultural influence is also a factor. And our culture has established a norm to discourage disclosing one's pregnancy until the first trimester passes. Have you ever thought about why? The truth is, it's because miscarriage is common and although people aren't often conscious of what they're saying, it's as though the message is this: "Your child might die, so don't tell people until that's less likely." The truth is, everyone will die, and if a child makes it past the first trimester there are no guarantees they will have a live birth. And if a child makes it to birth, we have no guarantee of decades with one's offspring. How long must someone live before we celebrate them? I have a friend who miscarried at nine weeks and another who lost a child at 13 weeks. My cousin miscarried at 21 weeks, and my aunt had a stillbirth at 40 weeks. One of my friends lost her child at two years old. Another friend lost her son at 19 years old. I don't want to be quiet about my child's existence because they might not live as long as someone else. Instead, I want to live life fully with my beloved child for as long as they are present.[xxvii]

To live life fully with your child for as long as he or she is present is possible in a public or a private way. Women have expressed how, following a miscarriage, they "rejoiced with trembling." Every mother will know best how to value the life of her pre-born child.

As pro-life parents, we honor the lives of all children, whether born or pre-born, no matter how long or short their lives are. No life is too short to be celebrated or grieved.

Infinitely valuable

In previous chapters, we discussed that every child is created in God's image, the *imago Dei*. Therefore, all pre-born children, born children, teens, and adults are image-bearers, which is critical to the pro-life position. Everything we believe about pre-born children flows from the knowledge that they have infinite value in God's eyes, so we must also value them in this way.

In the context of losing children during pregnancy, this knowledge tells us that each time a baby dies, an image-bearer is lost. No worldview comprehends the extent of this loss more than a Christian worldview, and if we subscribe to this, we must acknowledge all losses as such. Each parent who loses their child does not grieve the same way. Many women have shared that the loss of children at different stages of pregnancy impacted them in different ways, but all of these children *were* grieved.

Awareness about the grief resulting from losing

one's child during pregnancy has been increasing, both in pro-life communities and the broader culture. On the one hand, we can see this as a positive development. On the other hand, it can easily leave us feeling conflicted when, at the same time, children's lives are intentionally being ended through abortion.

Dr. Abernathy explains this exceptionally well.

> It's impossible to validate the loss and grief that we face when we lose a child to miscarriage without acknowledging the humanity and life that existed. And if what I mourn is the loss of a human child's life, abortion is taking the life of a human child. Naming the child and otherwise acknowledging this was an irreplaceable son or daughter reminds women who lose children by choice of what they have willingly done. This truth is not a pleasant message for post-abortive mothers.
>
> On the other hand, denying this truth is a huge slap in the face to grieving moms. If all I lost was a "potential person"—basically I am just disappointed that the pregnancy didn't end with a full-term baby. In that case, miscarriage is just a temporary bummer and "better luck next time." It denigrates our grief and pain and for no other reason than it makes society feel better about disposing of children at will.
>
> Lies told to enable evil toward unborn children

also hurt those who love (and lose) these babies. It is just another bonus gift from the culture of death.[xxviii]

In other words, it's either/or. Either pre-born children are human, and losing them is an enormous loss, or they are not human, and losing them is no big deal. We can't have it both ways. Science teaches that human parents can only have human offspring. Aborted children share their humanity with miscarried and stillborn children, and *all children* have infinite value as image-bearers. Our words, actions, and prayers must consistently reflect this.

None of us can do this perfectly, but this knowledge should not prevent us from learning and trying. For example, while writing this chapter, we used the term "pregnancy loss" many times. However, the more we learned, the more we realized that this doesn't do justice to the pain or the gaping hole that losing a child during pregnancy leaves. The parents we spoke with didn't just lose a pregnancy; they lost their baby. They weren't talking about missing their pregnancy but about missing their son or daughter. That's when we noticed that abortion clinics also use the term "pregnancy loss," fitting neatly with their view that the pre-born aren't human yet. We felt the need to correct our terminology to reflect the humanity and value of the pre-born *and* to honor the countless experiences of those who were left with the profound pain of losing a child during pregnancy.

Back to the basics

Our culture seems to understand that a pregnancy, when wanted, involves a baby. Thus, when a wanted pregnancy ends with miscarriage or stillbirth, it is usually treated as the loss of a child. Unfortunately, many Christians have been slow to recognize that each time a pre-born baby dies during pregnancy, someone loses their child. Even those who recognize this truth aren't always quick to express it, perhaps because it feels awkward or uncomfortable.

This discomfort may result from previous generations not viewing pre-born children as fully human due to a lack of scientific knowledge. Additionally, hardship and uncertain circumstances led people to not view their pre-born child as a member of the family until, at the very least, he or she had been born. Going further back in time, many babies did not receive a name until their first birthday due to high infant mortality rates. The oldest part of a local cemetery bears testimony to this: while walking along its paths, we saw many small headstones that were merely marked "Infant" together with a surname. Today, we deal with the remnants of those practices. When referring to our pre-born children, well-meaning elderly people have told us that "you don't have a baby until you hold it in your arms!" There appears to be a hesitancy to affirm the existence of a pre-born child to diminish the hurt in case the baby dies.

Once, after a presentation, a frail elderly lady came forward and said that when she watched the abortion video we showed, she couldn't help but think of her stillborn baby. "It's been decades," she shared. "My husband took it away and buried it somewhere; I don't know where. That's what we did back then. But I've never forgotten him." Not giving the baby a name did not take away her pain or erase his memory. The baby has continued to be a part of her for who he was: her son, a human being.

We can look back with compassion rather than judgment, learn from the past, and resolve to set aside our discomfort, awkwardness, and misguided traditions. Moving forward, let's be grounded and guided by foundational truths: the facts about when human lives begin and their value as created by God. These truths will validate the grief over the loss of children during pregnancy. These truths will impact what we communicate about life and loss to our children. In turn, we hope our children will grow up knowing that very young children matter very much, regardless of how long they've lived.

6

Responding to Infertility

Children are a blessing. Perhaps you have to remind yourself of this truth when you are severely sleep-deprived in the newborn stage, when your toddler colors on freshly painted walls with permanent markers, when a child continues to exhibit challenging behavior, or when your teen is giving you lots of reasons to spend more time in prayer. Perhaps that's precisely one of the ways children are a blessing: they provide us with countless opportunities to face our shortcomings, confess our sins, and rely on God. While the culture often sees children as an inconvenience, Psalm 127 tells us that they are a heritage of the Lord. To be a joyful mother of children is described as a blessing. Remarkably, the Bible refers to a woman becoming pregnant as having been visited by the Lord. It is undeniably biblical to celebrate the gift of children.

What about the many women who don't receive this particular gift?

This struggle is not new to our day and age. One must only read the Old Testament to know that women throughout all of human history have faced childlessness, and that struggle is often marked with deep, heart-wrenching pain. Sarah, Rachel, and Hannah, along with other women in Bible times, experienced similar anguish and bore the heavy weight of not having children. Times may have changed, but human struggles have not.

When talking with women about their personal experiences, we decided to use the term "infertility" to refer to anyone who struggled with conceiving or carrying children–not only those who haven't experienced pregnancy at all. Many moms may be able to relate to parts of this chapter, while others have no personal experience with infertility. Either way, it is a topic pro-life women cannot avoid.

Perhaps you wonder how this relates to raising our children pro-life. We've written about the importance of creating a family culture in which each human life is valued, honored, and celebrated as a gift from God. However, it is equally important to think about how we respond when these gifts are withheld from us or the people around us. We must learn and model humility in the face of hardship, especially when there are no easy answers.

A pro-life worldview makes all the difference. Since we recognize the value of all image-bearers, this includes those who struggle to have children. By our actions, even more so than our words, our children will learn how to have compassion for others in their pain. We must also be guided by truth when moral questions arise. That's why this chapter is found in a pro-life guide for moms. If we want to raise our children pro-life, we need to be prepared to teach truth, show love, and model sensitivity when it involves infertility as well.

The stories women shared with us

Just like there is no way of understanding the pain of those who have lost children unless you are one of them, there is no way of understanding the pain of those who face infertility unless you are one of them. For this reason, we wanted to include the voices of women walking this road. Hopefully, their stories will help us understand infertility better and teach us also to bear this burden together.

Sophia: "I feel as if everyone can recognize that the struggle with infertility is a difficult one. At the same time, if you haven't had to walk this path, it is impossible for you to truly understand the depth of grief that comes along with it. I struggled with how deeply I felt the loss of biological children that I only ever had in my dreams."

Christina: "I felt like, in a sense, I had lost a child. This child never existed, so I guess I was grieving a dream and hope."

Jessica: "You mourn the loss of all the dreams and hopes you had for a family. As a woman, you grieve the dreams of being pregnant, having the baby shower, buying maternity clothes, and watching your body change and grow. You grieve when you reach new steps in your journey, whether that's walking into a fertility clinic, starting treatments, coming to terms with the fact that you won't be able to have biological children, or coming to the decision to adopt."

Lauren: "Being a mother has been my dream for as long as I can remember...It never really hit until after we were married for a year and our friends started having babies. Then it really hit, and I knew something was wrong. We went through all kinds of tests, but nothing showed up. It was all unexplained. Knowing it is possible, but it's just not happening is very stressful because each month is another disappointment."

It was very humbling to realize that we can never fully comprehend the depth of the pain that infertility brings. We are grateful that these stories provide a glimpse into a world inaccessible to many of us. They allow us to grow in compassion and increase our ability to speak with sensitivity when communicating about infertility to our children. There is so much to learn.

Not everyone receives the same gifts

While each woman's journey is deeply personal, themes emerged in the feelings they expressed to us, such as the pain resulting from not having the marital union blessed with children or the struggle of not living up to the standard of being a family. Some feel more anguish about the former, while others struggle predominantly with the latter. Paige wrote, "It is difficult to see everyone having kids, and you are just waiting on the sidelines."

Ironically, it is precisely in communities where children are highly valued that couples facing infertility may find themselves feeling alienated and alone. Kelly described this as incredibly painful on the one hand and a blessing on the other hand.

It's painful because it's somehow an assumption that when you marry, you will have children (and quickly) and a lot of children. The majority of women in my community are defined by their motherhood, and that is the number one thing they talk about: being pregnant, having and raising children, their children having children, etc. However, it is a blessing because our family has welcomed us into their children's lives, and we both have roles where we can nurture and be part of raising the next generation.

As pro-life parents, we should be mindful to avoid the assumption that all Christians marry and have children. Dr. Karen Swallow Prior makes this point powerfully while reflecting on her experience with infertility.

> God's design for the family–the fruitful marriage between a man and a woman, the union of two image bearers that brings forth more image bearers–is mysterious, wonderful, and good. To desire such is good. Both marriage and children are God's good gifts. But to assume that God will give certain gifts is not good. Nor is it good to cultivate within the church the presumption that God is going to give his gifts to everyone.[xxix]

How should we walk with our friends who face infertility, and what do we model to our children?

Support from the community

As with the loss of children, women going through infertility mentioned how their (church) community responded in both heartwarming and hurtful ways. Grace wrote that "the issue of infertility is often skimmed over," while others appreciated the way their pastor prayed for those who are childless. Below are some examples to help us emulate the good and avoid the bad.

Several people mentioned that being acknowledged on Mother's Day or Father's Day was meaningful to them. Jessica wrote:

> This past Mother's Day, I expected it to be lonely, but so many people messaged me and said they were praying for me. God reminded me that I am not alone.

She was not the only one. Kelly shared the following:

> We sometimes get texts, cards, flowers, or small gifts on Mother's and Father's Day. An acknowledgment that those days are hard for us goes a long way. Being invited to be part of family celebrations, though difficult for us sometimes, is also appreciated. Getting invited to Grandparent Days by our nieces' and nephews' kids is special, too.

Christina echoed these feelings, being grateful for:

those who reach out on Mother's Day to let me know they were thinking of me or to acknowledge me. I felt my grief was validated when people would give me grace and not expect me to be at every baby shower or would give me a day or two to process their happy news about a new baby on the way, rather than surprise me with the news in public.

Almost all the women mentioned the latter. A pregnancy announcement as a big surprise is painful, especially in a larger group, since it can bring up many emotions that cannot be dealt with in that context. Paige: "Finding out [about someone's pregnancy] in a crowd when you've had a bad day is not nice. Even on a good day, it's like a punch to the gut, and it's very hard to hold those feelings down for a night. Then, when you come home, you don't feel that you can grieve properly because you have pushed the feelings down for so long."

Many articulated that they felt the most supported when they sensed that people were there for them, ready to listen, and loving them through their struggle. "It was like, I see you," Lindsey wrote. It validated her grief.

What would be helpful?

A recurring theme in the submissions we received is that people, while meaning well, can be insensitive with their words. Many have no personal experience with infertility to reflect on and learn from, lack awareness of how to talk about infertility, and consequently blunder through these situations like a bull in a china shop. The good news is that we can all learn to do better. A hurting woman generally doesn't need our words in the first place; she needs our support most of all. Sometimes, this means vocalizing our support, but we shouldn't talk just to fill the space. The best thing Job's friends did for him in his agony was to show up and be silent. (Later, when they spoke, their words were not helpful.)

An important piece of advice we received was that if there are childless couples in your family or community, know that this is rarely by choice.[5] If only we could remember those words every time we were in a conversation, we would be much more careful with what we say. Moreover, if we follow that advice, we will avoid hurting almost everyone. Those who are childless by choice can hardly be offended if we keep a careful guard over the words that leave our mouths, and those who are not childless by choice won't be hurt by words we didn't say.

---

[5] While writing this book, it came to our attention that there is an increase in couples intentionally remaining childless for a variety of reasons. For the purpose of this conversation surrounding infertility, we are not referring to them. If this applies to a couple you know, they'll likely be open about this decision, and you may want to have a different conversation with them than with those experiencing infertility.

Every woman mentioned the power of listening. Simply *listen*. Listen to what your friend says, and respect her if she responds, "I can't talk about it right now." Lindsey shared that before kids, it was often too painful to talk about infertility. It also opened up the possibility that she would have to process more painful comments. Looking back, she realized that most of her family didn't ask how they were doing and were perhaps afraid to. However, "that simple question would have been appreciated, and we could have chosen whether or not we wanted to share on that particular day...it seemed [that] they didn't care because they never bothered to ask how we were."

Another suggestion was that it's okay to acknowledge childlessness. We must remember that acknowledgment is distinct from offering placating statements. It's certainly not asking insensitive questions to garner information. Kelly wrote, "Do not ask 'whose fault' it is. It is neither's fault but a burden they share."

Many of us who have not experienced infertility are not comfortable talking about it, but we want to appear empathetic. There is a growing societal desire, which is especially visible on social media, to express our sentiments on many different topics, contribute, and 'fill the void.' Increasingly, we are uncomfortable with silence and often rush to speak when words are unnecessary. The other extreme, however, is to say nothing at all. Kelly, when reflecting on the fact that the elders of the church she and her husband attend have never asked questions about their infertility, wrote poignantly: "Believe me, we're even more aware of our childlessness than you are. Although it may be difficult to ask or pray about, not saying anything to us is even more difficult."

We have written much about guarding our tongue, but how does this translate into raising our kids pro-life? Be mindful not only of how you speak *to* couples suffering through infertility and miscarriage but doubly careful of how you speak *about* them. Children learn by example, and if our children hear us speak with compassion and grace, hopefully, they will speak that way in the future. Monica wrote positively about friends who talked with their children about these struggles:

> Their little girl often would pray for us. "I'm going to pray that God will give Chris and Monica a baby to love." This is something she learned from listening to her parents pray for us and others [who were] going through the same thing. If I could encourage families to do one thing for those suffering from infertility, I would ask them to pray, to encourage their kids to pray, and to model it as parents.

Other women echoed this. "Pray for us, that we might have children," one wrote. "But also pray that we might have strength for each day."

A woman is more than her ability to bear children

The accounts of those who've faced infertility are a telling indication that, in communities where children and the role of mothers are highly valued, women are often valued based on their ability to produce and nurture a family. Unconsciously, many have placed this expectation on themselves. Grace wrote, "As a woman with infertility, I questioned everything about myself and the value I had." Kelly confirmed this, saying she often felt she was "not a complete woman."

Sophia articulated these feelings as well, writing:

> Children should be valued highly; I would never want to act like this is a problem. The issue is how women are expected to fill a specific role within a specific time frame without proper recognition that this is not possible for everyone.

It's not wrong for women to find fulfillment in being mothers, but it *is* wrong for us to place that expectation on others. Our value is not found in what we can do (ability) or in what we are (role) but rather in *who we are* (image-bearer). Just like the preborn, our value comes from our Creator.

Women without children are complete women. Natalie writes, "Infertility does not define me. And I don't believe it should. See me for who I am, not who I'm not." As pro-life moms, let's support all our sisters and celebrate them for who they are. As Solomon writes in the book of Ecclesiastes, there is a time to weep and a time to laugh. We weep when they weep and rejoice when they rejoice. These times are opportunities to come together as pro-life families.

Called to adoption

For some, being childless may mean being called to something other than biological parenthood. Monica writes about facing infertility with her husband, considering fertility treatments, and prayerfully deciding to pursue adoption. "This partly comes from the strongly held pro-life belief that all human beings not only deserve life but also have worth and value." She advocates for a change in the language regarding adoption and a greater respect for birth mothers.

> In a community that regards itself as very pro-life, we were disappointed at how negatively birth moms are thought of. In our minds, our child's birth mom is a hero, and I will only speak of her in the absolute highest of terms. Because children are so highly valued in our communities, and because family is so important, I don't think many of my pro-life family or friends really understand the desperate circumstances that many women facing an unplanned pregnancy are in.

> There is no right or wrong answer to whether

couples should pursue adoption when ethical fertility treatments don't result in pregnancy. What matters most is perspective. Monica makes this point as well:

> Honestly, a key to joyfully facing infertility has been conscious reminders over and over of God's ultimate control over absolutely everything, including our infertility and how and when He grew our family. An eternal perspective changed everything about our difficult circumstances.

Other moms who went the adoption route spoke about seeing God's hand in how their child was brought into their family. Paige wrote, "Looking back now, I know our son we adopted had to be with us, and his birth mom thinks the same." Lindsey expressed it as follows,

> We didn't want our child to be forced into existence, if you will, and adoption had been in our hearts for months or even years. We felt that with adoption, a child could truly be given to us. This was all confirmed when our baby's birth mother handed him to us.

We asked for examples of thoughtful things their community did for them. Monica wrote:

> A huge way we were supported was when our friends got together and pooled cash for our

adoption fund. None of them had a ton of money, but they gave generously and anonymously, and it just felt amazing. Money was definitely a barrier for us in terms of adoption. The fact that they just dropped off an envelope of money showed how much they cared. When our baby joined our family, we experienced a crazy outpouring of love, well-wishes, and joy that we *totally* never expected.

What a beautiful way for a pro-life community to live out its convictions, affirming the value of a little child and rejoicing with this couple as they rejoiced.

In Vitro Fertilization

When pregnancy doesn't happen naturally, the medical world offers a wide variety of paths to pursue, from NaPro technology to hormone treatments to artificial reproductive technologies such as in vitro fertilization (IVF). From an ethical perspective, how far is too far? Do certain procedures contradict the pro-life worldview because of the loss of human life that is involved?

Infertility can make pro-lifers waver in their convictions. For couples desiring children, it may be tempting to follow the medical route, no matter the cost. "What else are we going to do?" a couple commented. "Not have kids?" Another friend agreed, explaining that her experience with infertility was so challenging that she wouldn't have the heart to tell anyone else they can't do whatever it takes to get pregnant.

For pro-lifers who do have children, it can be difficult to disagree with a procedure that may allow your family members or friends to have biological children. "It feels cruel," I once expressed to my friend whose desire to have children had gone unfulfilled, "when you've never faced infertility yourself to then disagree with IVF. It's like I'm condemning someone's last chance at having a biological child." She completely disagreed:

> Infertility is hard, really hard. But while I would encourage those who have not walked this path to empathize with others, we who are faced with infertility do not have a monopoly on suffering. Suffering doesn't give us license to do whatever we want to fix it. Just like you can say that a pregnant woman may not choose abortion in her difficult circumstances, you should be able to say that a woman facing infertility may not choose an option that will put the lives of at least 70% of her children created in the lab at risk of death.

That brings us back to who the pre-born are, including tiny one-celled embryos created in a lab. They are unique, living, human individuals with intrinsic value, created in the image of God. If our actions can directly and intentionally cause death to small human beings, we can't morally consent to that course of action.

We are thankful for each of the children who

were safely born after being conceived through IVF. How we treat people does not depend on the circumstances of their conception. Their life is infinitely valuable. The same is true for millions of children who didn't make it to birth due to the manner in which they were conceived. One of the moms experiencing infertility wrote, "Yes, we desired the gift of children–but we weren't willing to create life in ways that we believed risked harm to that life."

If we are serious about pro-life convictions, we must be willing to take a serious and critical look at artificial reproductive technologies that endanger human lives. We should be willing to discuss and research these with our teenagers or young adults. As a helpful resource, we've included an article published by The Gospel Coalition entitled "Breaking Evangelicalism's Silence on IVF" as an appendix. We also recommend the book *Conceived by Science: Thinking Carefully and Compassionately about Infertility and IVF* by Stephanie Gray Connor.

A different calling

In *Called to Childlessness: The Surprising Ways of God,* Dr. Prior wrote:

> God's model for the family is beautiful and good, the very picture of the union of Christ and his church: the fruitful marriage of one man and one woman.
>
> Yet, the church often doesn't know what to do

with those who—whether by circumstance, conscience, choice or simply through the brokenness of creation—fall outside the mold that shapes this ideal of family life.

There is an unspoken assumption that this failure to fit the pattern is just that—a failure. To be sure, sometimes we break the mold by our choices, even our sins. But ours is a God of great imagination and infinite surprises. He sometimes calls us out of the standard mold and into a new one.[xxx]

For those of us who have children, it might be hard to imagine not pursuing parenthood in other ways when it does not come naturally. However, some women are given peace about their childlessness, especially when trusting in God's sovereignty. Natalie testified:

> So often, the grief is focused on, and that's to be expected. But if we believe it's God's plan, and that we don't deserve children, and that He may have a much greater plan for us, there is so much peace and joy to be enjoyed. Most people are completely shocked at this. This baffles me. We serve an awesome God Who knows what's best for us. We need daily lessons in trust and faith in Him.

Women spoke about inwardly reflecting on whether they were listening to what God called them to do and living to His glory. That is His mandate for each of us; it does not depend on having children. Some may be able to serve God in unique ways without children. Dr. Prior reiterated this point:

> The contributions God has allowed me to make to the church and the world are contributions specific to being a woman, and, further, a woman without children.
>
> I believe that the church and the world need more of the particular gifts that infertile (and childless and unmarried) women (and men) can offer. I can't help but wonder how different the church and the world would look if infertility were viewed not as a problem to be solved, but a calling to serve God and meet the needs of the world in other ways.[xxxi]

What does this mean for pro-life parents?

We hope we've done justice to the experiences of the many couples who shared their stories with us. What does this mean for pro-life families? How can we take everything we've learned about infertility and apply it to raising the next generation pro-life?

We've passed on the dos and don'ts of walking alongside friends and families who face infertility. All of this boils down to one word: compassion.

The Latin root of compassion is *pati*, which

means "to suffer." The prefix *com-* means "with." In other words, to have compassion means *to suffer with*. To be pro-life means *to suffer with*. To raise our children pro-life, then, is to teach compassion. How better to teach it than to model it? How better to model it than *to suffer with*?

The hardships written about in Chapters 5 and 6, and the way women spoke about them in light of God's leading in their lives, made us think of a well-known poem often quoted by Corrie ten Boom (1892-1983). After World War II, Corrie traveled around the world sharing the Gospel while speaking about the suffering she experienced in a Nazi concentration camp and the loved ones she lost during that time. She often quoted "The Weaver" by Grant Tullar. We thought it was worth including.

The Weaver[xxxii]

My life is but a weaving
betwixt my God and me;
I do not choose the colors
He worketh steadily.
Sometimes He weaveth sorrow,
and I in foolish pride
Forget He sees the upper
and I the underside.

Not till the loom is silent
and the shuttles cease to fly
Will God unfold the pattern
and explain the reason why.
For the dark threads are as needful
in the Weaver's skillful hand
As the threads of gold and silver
in the pattern He has planned.

Grant Tullar (1869-1950)

7

To Be Christian Is To Be Pro-Life

Have you ever looked at our secular culture and felt that you don't fit in? As a parent, have you wondered how to raise children in a society so hostile to truth? We've certainly asked these questions, and based on countless conversations, many others have as well. This reality is causing moms and dads to ask, "How do I ensure that I don't lose my kids to this culture?" Encouragingly, the result is that parents are intentionally raising their children with biblical values and teaching Christian apologetics. They're applying a Christian perspective to *all* areas of life, and this is good news.

If this is the case, what is the reason for this book? Isn't Christianity enough to combat the culture of death? Yes, it is. Most Christians are certainly pro-life and affirm the value of pre-born children within their family, and that is objectively good. Yet, for many families, addressing abortion is not included in those efforts. Why is this?

If we love children and live in child-loving communities, abortion seems far removed from our lives. We may snuggle a precious newborn and wonder why so many people insist on their right *not* to experience that. We can't fathom pulling precious little children apart nor fully comprehend the evil of the actual abortion practice. Most of us don't try, either, and to be fair, who would want to?

We've been told by fellow moms more than once that they "don't go there." "I can't dwell on awful things like that," you may say, "so I'll hug my kids harder and ensure they're safe." Bring on the hugs–we're with you there! God gave us our children; therefore, our primary responsibility is their physical and spiritual well-being. We must undoubtedly create a culture of life in our homes.

Some argue for a purely positive approach, in which we only teach what is good and beautiful. This is a good foundation, and affirming those values is very important. Yet, more is needed. How do we know?

In Matthew 22, a lawyer asked the Lord Jesus which commandment was greatest. He replied:

> Thou shalt love the Lord thy God with all thy heart, and with all thy soul, and with all thy mind. This is the first and great commandment. And the second is like unto it, Thou shalt love thy neighbour as thyself (37-39).

He concluded: "On these two commandments hang all the law and the prophets" (40).

Jesus makes it clear that everything God requires can be summarized by one word: love. The apostle Paul expands on this by saying that no matter the gifts, understanding, knowledge, or faith, we are nothing if love is missing. Love for God will produce love for our neighbor. The Lord Jesus' conclusion naturally flows out of the commandments to love: the law given to Moses and everything the prophets taught fit into these categories.

Why is this important? Many view the Ten Commandments given at Sinai as negative prohibitions and avoid reading the prophets who, according to them, sound like doomsday preachers. Most people would prefer to focus on love, not sin. But in His conclusion, Jesus unmistakably connects the two. Those who love God also hate sin. Those who love their neighbor will hate the harm done to them. Therefore, Christians are not only pro-life but also anti-abortion.

The Heidelberg Catechism affirms this when expounding on the commandment "Thou shalt not kill." It is not good enough to refrain from killing others. We must also prevent others from being harmed as much as we can!

> Question 107: But is it enough that we do not kill any man in the manner mentioned above? Answer: No, for when God forbids envy, hatred, and anger, He commands us to love our neighbor as ourselves; to show patience, peace, meekness, mercy, and all kindness towards him, and prevent his hurt as much as in us lies; and that we do good even to our enemies.[xxxiii]

Throughout the ages, faithful Christians have always opposed the mistreatment of their neighbors and have been known for their acts of mercy. The early church in Rome rescued unwanted infants that had been abandoned and left to die on the city walls, raising them as their own, often illegally and at great risk to themselves. Motivated by Christian conviction, the abolitionist movement in Great Britain accomplished the unthinkable by tirelessly campaigning against and successfully banning the slave trade. People who loved the Lord pioneered the Sunday school movement, Christian schools, hospitals for the underprivileged, orphanages, soup kitchens, shelters, rescue missions, and relief agencies. They served the Lord in serving their neighbors.

A study of 2000 years of Christian history, found in the well-researched and beautifully illustrated "The Christians" series by the late Ted Byfield, provides many examples of people who knew their Creator and actively valued the lives of all those He created. As Jonathon Van Maren writes,

> Wherever human beings created in God's image were threatened, it was the churches, first, who responded with compassion and assistance. As the preacher Charles Haddon Spurgeon once thundered, "The God that answers by orphanages, let Him be Lord!"[xxxiv]

This is entirely scriptural. Who hasn't heard of the parable of the good Samaritan? The Lord Jesus makes it clear that loving our neighbor is not only *respecting* his life but also *objecting* to the harm that might befall him and *showing mercy* when he has become the victim of those who do not value his life. If we must help an adult man found beaten and bloody on the side of the road, isn't the same action expected of us when it concerns a tiny child who will otherwise become a bloody victim of abortion? The pre-born are our neighbors, too.

The difficulty, of course, is that we do not come across aborted children in the same way that we might meet a neighbor in need, and because of this, abortion often isn't on our radar. Stephanie Gray Connors addresses this when she writes,

> Just as the Good Samaritan "saw" with his eyes, and his heart, the plight of his neighbour, we should pray "that we may see" the plight of our pre-born neighbours just as Jesus sees it. We should allow ourselves to come face-to-face with their broken bodies and allow their dismembered limbs to communicate to us what their silent screams could not. We should pray to "see" their beauty and fragility, and the corresponding destruction of what abortion did to them, so as to respond with the broken heart that God Himself responds with.[xxxv]

We will never be able to see abortion victims in the same way that God sees every single one of them. We can, however, ask Him to burden our hearts with the plight of children He knit together perfectly in their mother's womb.

Creating a culture of life

Recently, a friend told me that a speaker asked

a question that had made her think: "If your neighbors cared about abortion as much as you did, what would it look like?" It's a powerful way to take inventory of our lives. Would it be attending the March for Life once a year or participating in 40 Days for Life? Would it be a prayer at the dinner table or a monthly donation to a pro-life organization? Would it be anything or nothing at all?

In this chapter, we wanted to explore the concept of creating a culture of life in our homes. Yet, the more we thought about it, the more we realized that what we were describing was simply a Christian way of living, where being pro-life isn't just an activity or even good apologetics but a fundamental value. It is not a checklist of things we must do but a core belief from which our actions flow. To be Christian is to be pro-life.

Why do we not see that reflected in the church in general? We are *not* saying that there aren't Christians living out their values. Many people are burdened for the pre-born, which is evident in their lives. Yet, conversations have made it clear to us that a large number of Christians make a distinction between being Christian and being pro-life. We've heard "the pro-lifers" used as a term to describe those who are actively engaged in the fight for life. But shouldn't all Christians be engaged in that fight? If every church community suddenly began to prioritize a Christian response to abortion, would our culture notice? Would it make a difference for pre-born children?

It is difficult to hear the word action in relation to being pro-life and not think that we are telling you to sign up for pro-life activism on the streets. Certainly, if that is how you feel, your local pro-life chapter will gladly accept a willing "yes." However, action does not equal activism; it does not mean you *must* stand on the street or do public outreach. Action in our homes begins with a quiet yes– a decision that today, you will remember the pre-born in your prayers. If this is new for you, your children may notice and ask you about it. Take this as an open door, and see where it leads.

Being actively pro-life might not mean doing one specific thing, but it does mean that there is always some kind of pro-life action. We must actively seek the good of the pre-born in our words, prayers, and deeds. What if children in pro-life homes feel, hear, and see that abortion weighs on their parents' hearts, something they're seeking to address in whichever way they can? Would they not grow up thinking that inaction in response to injustice is simply not an option?

Sociological research supports the positive effect that being actively pro-life has on the convictions of our (older) children. Dr. Munson found that many become firmly pro-life and involved *after* attending rallies or marches. Even those who were already pro-life found that the moral shock of what abortion is did not hit home until after some level of engagement.[xxxvi] We've seen this effect numerous times, for example, when teenagers from pro-life families attend a pro-life event and suddenly become passionately involved. In other words, participating in pro-life activities with our family reinforces the culture of life we create in our homes.

It starts with our hearts

In a conversation about her book *Fighting for Life*, Lila Rose was asked why she decided to be so open about her personal life. She responded:

> When I look at what really is going to make a difference in the world... if we not only want to end abortion but if we want to build a culture that is truly pro-life, it requires deep inner transformation and change, as much as it requires us being activists in the culture around us, fighting for what's right...I really believe that if we want to change the world around us, we have to allow ourselves to be changed, and obviously that's by God's grace.[xxxvii]

Perhaps that strikes you as a bridge too far. *Are you telling me that not only am I supposed to start talking about human life in the womb and abortion in the world, but that I also need personal change?* We cannot tell you what kind of transformation you might need; perhaps you're one of the few people who don't. If we know our hearts just a little bit, it is evident that our default position is to be inward-focused or even self-centered. We can resolve to do what is right, but we may also need inner change. Maybe we need more compassion. After all, how can we genuinely care for pre-born children and broken men and women if that doesn't flow from a heart full of love?

What if we take it one step further? How can we hug our teenage son or daughter dealing with an unplanned pregnancy if we still think we're better than others? Do we teach our children that home is the safest place to go should this be their situation, or do they hear us talk negatively about others in similar situations?

In high school, my homeroom teacher said someone had requested to share a message with the class. One of my friends stood up and stumblingly shared that he wanted to take responsibility for his actions: his girlfriend was pregnant. It was a vulnerable moment for everyone, but it was orchestrated this way so there was no gossip or hearsay but an open conversation, the opportunity to ask questions, and the start of a beautiful process where our class rallied around very young parents and their baby. It was one of the most memorable experiences of my high school years, and our graduation together was all the more special. I learned that forgiveness is not an empty promise when we are commanded to confess our sins. Where sin had become evident, grace abounded.

Maybe you've never considered that this might happen in your family. However, if we know ourselves as fallen people in need of grace, we also know that our teenagers can make mistakes that may lead to pregnancy. Like Bryan Kemper, whom we mentioned previously, we must be ready to face unplanned pregnancies with compassion and care—not judgment and condemnation—when they happen in our families and larger communities. "I love you" are powerful words.

For a teenage girl or young adult, becoming pregnant while unmarried might feel like the biggest mistake she ever made, the kind that you can't come back from. Conservative communities, likely unintentionally, may send this message by how they respond to such a pregnancy. Could we respond to this in another way? It is true that extramarital sex is not according to God's good plan and that our children will need to repent and seek forgiveness for this sin if they commit it. As we have mentioned earlier, it is also the only sin that may lead to new life, and that life is a gift from above. The Bible tells us that "the wages of sin is death but the gift of God is eternal life through Jesus Christ, our Lord" (Rom. 6:23). In the case of pregnancy resulting from sex outside of marriage, the wage of sin is a baby. Could anything be more symbolic of redemption than a new life?

That's not all. In a culture saturated with abortion-positive messages, it's easy to think of a very young embryo as "just a bunch of cells." In the panic of finding out about an unwanted pregnancy, how tempting would it be to tell yourself that "it's not really a baby yet"? Picturing their parents' pain and feeling their own shame, many Christian girls succumb to the lie that "getting it taken care of" will be better for everyone. In short, it may take a lot of courage not to abort, even (or especially!) inside pro-life circles. What if we change that? While we fight for little boys and little girls that the culture of death will otherwise destroy on the outside, let's make sure we contend for a culture in which every life is celebrated on the inside.

If you are a Bible-believing Christian, your identity is already pro-life. Throughout history, the actions of Christians have demonstrated that this is inherent to the Christian worldview. The Bible hasn't changed. Instead of dividing Christians into categories of "actively pro-life and passively pro-life" or "those who do pro-life work and those who don't," why don't we start recognizing that everyone has a role–because it's part of our identity? It's not just a calling for some but for all of us.

What being pro-life may look like

As an encouragement, we'd love to give you some examples of how this can play out differently in each of our lives. We asked permission to share these stories and used pseudonyms where requested.

André and Karyn's choices repeatedly show their identity. They have cared for homeless and pregnant women, mentored Christians struggling with infertility, suffered the loss of children during pregnancy, and opened their hearts to foster care and adoption when God placed it on their path. In their personal and professional lives, their actions speak volumes about being pro-life Christians.

Patrick and Miriam have a farm and are often extremely busy trying to keep the operation going while dealing with health challenges. Yet, whenever possible, they deliver fresh food to people in ministry and families with financial needs, even generously giving away their own harvest and canning stores. Their actions, baffling many, speak volumes about being pro-life Christians.

Many women face significant challenges to their health. Some conditions provide a legitimate excuse not to be involved in local and national endeavors for the pre-born. However, many women still choose to make a difference where they can. Sarah makes meals for families with newborns. Astrid maintains donor relations for a pro-life organization. While hospitalized for a week, Danielle organized a fundraiser for a pregnancy care center: "There was a need, and I had time and a phone." Maria calls and emails her local, provincial, and federal politicians about concerning pieces of legislation and reaches out to her friends and families to do the same. Despite chronic pain, she attends town hall meetings via Zoom and defends fundamental freedoms so that the pro-life movement can continue to be a voice for the pre-born. The actions of these women speak volumes about being pro-life Christians.

Matthias, Natalya, Benji, Iva, Seth, Jessalyn, Josiah, Rebekah, Justice, and Jonah are young people who faithfully engage in street outreach in our local community. Their families are involved with or supportive of pro-life work in some capacity. Their parents led by example while including their kids, and their actions have inspired more young people to join. In a society with low expectations for teens, these youths are raising the bar. Their countercultural actions speak volumes about being pro-life Christians.

We personally know over a dozen families who prioritize pro-life activities on their calendars. They've organized fundraisers, come to presentations, attended the March for Life, encouraged their kids to be involved, made care packages for moms with needs, and consistently brought all of these things to God in prayer over the years. Their family culture speaks volumes about being pro-life Christians.

When we consider the contributions of the people in these examples and the many others we have not mentioned, it provides a beautiful picture of what is accomplished when everyone with Christian convictions faithfully turns them into actions. Some actions may seem big; others may seem small. Some will be recognized–many will not–but ultimately, what matters is that we do them. In the words of J.R.R. Tolkien, "Deeds will not be less valiant because they are unpraised."

What about you?

Now is the time to ask what this means for you. What's your place? Where do you fit in? What can your family do? What *more* can your family do?

Since the Scriptures are inspired by God and command us to teach our children diligently, what does that look like in your home? If you believe that the Bible is true and has authority over your life, what does it mean when it tells us to love our neighbors as ourselves? As we continue to answer these questions in our lives and for our families, we hope you'll do the same for yours.

As you conclude this book, we pray that you will ask the Lord to show you the place He has for you and that your actions will speak volumes about being a pro-life Christian.

When your Christian worldview is applied to all areas of life, you join a growing movement of families worldwide who wish to take a stand by living pro-life and who are raising their children with these simple and beautiful truths. More than that, you're following in the footsteps of millions of Christians who have gone before us, finding great joy, even when it involves great sacrifice.

As Dr. George Grant wrote in his book *Third Time Around:*

> The pro-life movement is not a recent phenomenon or innovation. It is two thousand years old. You see, the pro-life movement was inaugurated on a rugged old cross, on a hill called Calvary—it is best known as Christianity. Caring for the helpless, the deprived, and the unwanted is not simply what we do. It is what we are. Always has been. Always will be.[xxxviii]

Acknowledgments

It took us many years to write this *Mom's Guide*, and there are easily as many people who have contributed to it as there were breaks from writing for births and babies and other endeavors that deserved our primary attention. To all those named and unnamed, thank you. We could not have written this book without you.

To our colleagues at the Canadian Centre for Bio-Ethical Reform: Your ongoing dedication to pre-born children inspires us to continue doing our part every day. The in-depth discussions about apologetics and moral dilemmas, coupled with your understanding of us as co-workers and very busy moms, *and* careful questions about when (or if) our book was (ever) going to be done, have helped our writing tremendously. It is an honor to be on the same team.

To the many families around us who are intentionally raising pro-life kids, and to the moms from whom we have learned so much of what we try to practice at home: we are very grateful.

To our publication team–thank you. You identified the need for this guide, provided endless guidance and support, and brought it through to publication. You are the dream team.

Countless people contributed in different ways to the writing and production process. We want to thank all our wonderful friends who helped in many different ways. You know who you are. While it may not have seemed world-changing, every kind deed meant the world to us. We are so privileged to be part of a large group of pro-life families who support each other and do life together. It is good to belong.

There were many instances as we wrote this book that we needed some immediate input. Many women (and some men) answered our calls and took the time to analyze and review certain lines and paragraphs. Since then, more people have joined the ranks, and each has provided invaluable feedback. To Katie Somers, Alanna Gomez, Jessi Corson, Justina Van Manen, Mikaela Sinke, Joop Buker, Caroline Heikoop, and Dad Sonnevelt: Thank you for reviewing our text. You refined our ideas and shaped much of what is here. A special thank you goes to Jacqueline Engelen, who accidentally became our editor by vocalizing her love for correcting incorrect English language and grammar usage. We appreciate you and the many hours spent on this project. All errors, of course, are our own.

To Alysha Joosse, dear friend, fellow mom, and talented photographer: You've given so many hours to the pro-life movement, always willing to run with another of our crazy staff photoshoot ideas together with your trusty sidekick. We appreciate you both. Thank you for the beautiful pictures.

To Sharon Grisnich: Not too long ago, we spent many hours drinking tea, talking, and sharing big ideas; I never dreamed that we would end up working together in this capacity. Your ability to turn a drawn-out voice note into a brilliant book cover is remarkable, and your patience with the process is commendable. Thank you for using your talent to create beauty.

To our husbands–if we had to list everything we are thankful for, we'd never get home on time. Thank you for believing in us to write *A Mom's Guide to Raising Pro-Life Kids*. Though we did, you are the unsung heroes. Your sacrifices for our families speak volumes about your convictions, and it is an enormous privilege to be doing pro-life work together, both in the culture and at home. We are thankful for our friendship and, as our kids put it, thankful "to be in a life together."

To our children, you are the reason we were able to write this book. It's taken us a long time to be able to say this, but it's finally done. Thank you for your patience, your permission to share some of our stories, and your never-ending faith in us. We love you. The Lord truly blessed us when He gave us each of you, and we are grateful to God for His help. We pray that He receives all the honor.

Appendix

Breaking Evangelicalism's Silence on IVF

By Matthew Lee Anderson and Andrew T. Walker

The quiet heartbreak and pain of infertility is well known to many evangelicals, whose aspirations to have a child have been frustrated for reasons they cannot understand or control. It is frequently a secret burden that couples carry, which only emerges into the open as they reveal their struggles to family, friends, and doctors.

The weight of infertility and the value of children has increasingly prompted infertile couples to pursue procreation by every means possible: artificial insemination, *in vitro* fertilization, and even surrogacy have all found their way into evangelical communities.

Yet while evangelicals have become increasingly aware of the emotional challenges infertility poses, we have not yet considered the hidden costs of our desperate pursuit of children through artificial reproductive technologies.

Few movies have brought those challenges into the open like Netflix's *Private Life* (warning: show contains explicit content). The film narrates the hope and heartbreak a couple experiences as they walk through various means of aiding conception, and the personal and relational distress that arises from their efforts. After receiving one final, disappointing report of failure, the husband callously asks his wife while lying in bed next to her, "Will we ever have sex again?" The wife, not surprisingly, denounces the question as self-interested and insensitive.

The moment poignantly captures how fertility treatments reconfigure how infertile couples sometimes experience their sexual lives together. Ironically, the couple had consigned sex to marriage's dustbin; the very act that might naturally generate children has been relegated to an inconvenient, cloying annoyance. What should be a source of joy and deep union has become a painful reminder of their frustrated desires.

For many evangelicals, though, the ethics of *in vitro* fertilization begins and ends at the question of how many embryos are created and what happens to them. Beyond this, many evangelicals do not even think *in vitro* fertilization is a "moral issue." Why would it be, when it seems to be simply a medical technology that helps couples satisfy their deep desires for what God has deemed good—namely, the birth of a child made in God's image? To say "no" to such technologies is, for many couples, equivalent to saying "no" to the satisfaction of their deepest, most heartfelt desires.

While not every couple experiences the direct marital hardship *Private Life* depicts, there are serious costs to and from accepting technologies that separate the "one flesh" union of husband and wife. We think those costs are high enough that evangelical couples and pastors should say no to *in vitro* fertilization. It's past time to break evangelicalism's silence about our complicity in the unethical circumstances that arise when sex and conception are divided.

Understanding *In Vitro* Fertilization

In Vitro Fertilization (IVF) is a process in which medical doctors create human life outside the boundaries of sexual intercourse. According to Pew, since 1996, more than 1 million babies in the United States—or 2 percent of children—have been born through some form of artificial reproductive technology.

IVF requires eggs and sperm to be harvested. For men, this often involves masturbation, but may also include surgical removal of sperm. The woman's ovaries are hormonally stimulated to harvest multiple eggs at once. Clinicians then create an embryo by fertilizing the egg in the lab, before transferring the embryo to the woman's uterus. (In intracytoplasmic sperm injections, which are increasingly common, doctors select a single sperm and inject it directly into the egg.) One cycle of IVF can produce multiple embryos, or only one. Even after transferrence, a woman's body can still reject the embryo. Embryos not transferred are usually stored.

While this process seems like a safe medical

treatment for infertility, moral questions abound. Questions about what happens to embryos, for instance, are paramount: The embryo is a *person*, and so deserves love and respect. If a couple opts to create many embryos, what happens to those who are not transferred? Is freezing them indefinitely, or giving them to research, just? Even if a couple *intends* to transfer every embryo they create, what happens if future events make that impossible? Some couples get pregnant naturally after undergoing IVF, or are otherwise prevented from following through on their intentions, leaving their embryos in frozen limbo.

Evangelical couples aware of such questions have increasingly opted to only create a single embryo at a time. Yet the separation of conception from sexual intercourse raises problems on its own, problems that outweigh any justification for using IVF to overcome infertility. To put our worry bluntly, God bound sex and procreation together in creation, and what God has joined together, no evangelical should separate.

Bible and IVF

For many Christians, Scripture's silence about IVF means that the only moral question is how we treat embryos created in the process. Such an argument, though, intrinsically undermines the *normativity* of Genesis 1 and 2 for both sexual ethics and also bioethics — a normativity that Jesus himself ratifies in Matthew 19:4. Genesis 1:26–28 clearly indicates human fertility has been folded by God into the structure of creation and into his providential plan for the earth's cultivation. And while Genesis 2:22–25 does not mention procreation directly, the interdependence of sex and generation is explicitly presumed. The man and woman cleave to each other and become "one flesh." But they do so only within a context already structured by kinship bonds established by procreation: "Therefore a man shall leave his father and his mother and hold fast to his wife, and they shall become one flesh." Sexual intercourse is inherently and intrinsically ordained by God toward procreation: A union that is "one flesh" cannot escape this reality, even if the couple chooses to deny it. To view this interdependency as simply contingent, rather than normative, radically undermines the place of Genesis 1–2 in both theological anthropology and ethics.

Such a principle is not, in this way, only founded on biology or considerations from natural law; it stands beneath the whole of how Scripture speaks about marriage, children, and God's action in bringing about both. The biological reality of procreation simply demonstrates how special and general revelation speak with one voice. Children are a heritage and gift from the Lord: we are "fearfully and wonderfully made" by God in the womb. Such divine action happens in and through the human act that is a union of unmediated love between the potential mother and father and no one else. In this way, exclusivity within human generation corresponds to the exclusivity of marriage.

The normative inter-relationship of marriage, sex, and procreation stands beneath Abraham's wrongness in turning to Hagar in attempting to bring about the fulfillment of God's promised gift of blessing (Gen. 16). It is not sexual intercourse *per se* that Abraham seeks, but an heir. Abraham's decision moves the continuation of the covenant outside of his union with Sarah, and in that way is nearer to surrogacy than to IVF. Yet in dividing what God holds together for the sake of bringing about the blessing on his own terms, Abraham enacts the same problem that besets contemporary artificial reproductive practices.

We think Scripture is unambiguous about the inextricable normative union of procreation and sex. What God has established in creation should be respected. We will elaborate on that principle by specifying four different concerns.

Four Concerns About IVF

1. **IVF Severs the Unified Goods of Marriage**

   In the first place, the practice of separating conception from sex in order to bring about a child risks reconfiguring evangelicalism's understanding of sex, marriage, and family. Dividing the natural and unified process of procreation into a variety of stages makes it more difficult to imagine why they were created together in the first place.

   The bifurcation between sex and procreation already has deep roots in our moral imagination. Fundamentally, IVF offers and reaffirms the same divide between sex and conception that hormonal contraception made plausible, even if it does so in the reverse way: Where contraception offers sex without conception, IVF offers conception without sex. But while many evangelicals would affirm the legitimacy of contraception, the ethic that stands beneath the division between procreation and sex permits many practices they would rightfully protest. Gay marriage, fornication, contraception, and IVF all sever the natural and creational link between sexual acts and the generation of human life.

The erosion of this link helps explain why the Christian sexual ethic retains less purchase culturally with each passing generation. If sexual pleasure and conception are not held together within marriage, they will not be held together outside of it.

2. **IVF Reconfigures Our Understanding of Human Life**

While those who pursue *in vitro* fertilization are often animated by love for each other, the specific acts that bring about human life are disconnected from the loving union that ordinary conception involves.

But this point introduces new factors into our understanding of where human life comes from. In ordinary acts of procreative love, there is no question who is conceiving the child: The process of generating life is begun and completed wholly by the couple. Third parties are only involved externally: They aid and support the process, and sometimes correct it, but they cannot in any material sense claim to be an originating agent in an infant's life.

The presence of multiple parties in conceiving life, though, introduces peculiar uncertainties and risks for the children who are born. Can we say that the married couple conceived this child, or the doctors? In cases of ordinary procreation, children might have complaints against their parents or God for how their life goes. But in cases of extracorporeal conception, such complaints might reasonably include the lab technicians materially involved in their conception. The diffusion of agents in creating human life that IVF demands risks diminishing the child's sense that they were "knit together in their mother's womb."

Moreover, IVF reconfigures how we think about the body and its reproductive capacities. IVF is *not* a medical treatment for infertility, but a way of sidestepping the appropriate use of one's own reproductive organs and the limits of one's own bodily life. Medicine is a practice ordered toward therapeutically restoring capacities to an individual's organic human life that have been lost due to illness, disability, disease, accident, or other disabling events. As reproductive systems are incomplete without a member of the other sex, their proper fulfillment happens in sexual intercourse.

But the "medical" interventions required for IVF are crucially distinct from those that would restore or repair the reproductive systems. For instance, women do not "use" their reproductive organs in having their eggs harvested. The interventions required for IVF don't accord with their reproductive system's design. To see this, consider a case where IVF is pursued because of male infertility; the woman's reproductive system is functioning properly in only generating one (presumably healthy) ovum every month. IVF artificially stimulates the woman's ovaries to produce multiple eggs concurrently, and then subjects her to an invasive procedure to harvest them. Neither of these acts can plausibly be described as "therapeutic" or remedial for her reproductive system. Even in cases where the woman's reproductive system is disordered, IVF does not fix the fundamental problem so much as attempt to sidestep it.

In this way, circumventing sex for the sake of conception outside the womb threatens to undermine the intelligible purposes of our bodily life. This is the force of the scene in *Private Life*: Aiming for children without sex changes the character of the latter, and with it the rest of our bodily life as well. IVF enshrines in the Christian moral imagination an attitude that, if applied consistently, would radically reconfigure not only our sexual ethics, but medical ethics as well.

3. **IVF Tampers with Human Life and Human Dignity**

The process of conceiving life in a lab establishes a principle of efficiency that intrinsically and inexorably inclines participants in the process toward weighing the value of persons based on the qualities of their lives.

In ordinary procreation, the human person emerges from a mysterious, invisible process of organic development. While we know from science what happens in the early days of conception, it is a work that remains hidden from the couple or any other human beings. Conception is an exceedingly fragile event, whether in the womb or the lab. But the doctor's presence within the process of forming human life practically demands grading embryos for their viability, and opting to "use" those that seem to show the best "quality." Such a tendency within the practice itself will make preimplantation genetic diagnosis almost an inevitable feature, especially as it becomes cheaper. As IVF is aimed at overcoming the inefficiencies of frustrated procreative efforts, the use of such screening measures will inevitably expand, as will the pressure on parents to employ them.

In this way, IVF as a practice orders our imaginations toward determining what types of human beings are the most likely to or capable of living a good life. Oliver O'Donovan (among others) has spoken of the distinct logic of begetting versus making, and the importance of the former to forming human life. When humans become comfortable *making* other humans, we will doubtlessly begin to construct them in the image of our own preferences and desires. Those conceived in a lab are fully made in God's image, but that doesn't diminish the rupture to our theological anthropology that IVF requires.

4. IVF Poses Risks to Women's Health

Finally, procreating human life is not only an immensely fragile process, but an exceedingly risky one as well. And the children created are subject to those risks. In the short term, pregnancies from artificial reproductive technologies are more likely to be subject to complications than through ordinary conception. The long-term effects of such treatments on children conceived through them are still wholly unknown. But those risks are even more pressing for women.

As mentioned above, the process of harvesting eggs is exceedingly invasive, and requires the non-therapeutic use of hormones. The long-term effects of this procedure are, as with children, disputable. But that's partially because fertility treatments are a lucrative industry, and there's systemic pressure to avoid closely considering such questions. As medical anthropologist Diane Tober admitted to *The Washington Post*, there are "no known risks [to fertility treatments] because no one has looked."

The double burden IVF places on women should be sufficient by itself for evangelicals to say no. Every woman risks her own health in generating human life. Yet the invasive, non-medical hormonal regime required for IVF doubles this risk. In this way, IVF extends the logic of hormonal contraception—which allows men to pursue their interests by disproportionately burdening women with the task of regulating their bodies—rather than requiring men to pursue the virtue of continence.

Other considerations could be brought forward

against IVF and its acceptance within evangelical communities. Such a practice increases the economic costs of generating life, which inherently limits it to upper-class households (or requires insurance or the state to fund it for low-income couples). As a practice, IVF has generated millions of embryo deaths — which raises questions about complicity in systems founded upon moral wrongs, even *if* an individual's couples intentions are "pure." And there are others.

Fundamentally, though, accepting the division between sex and conception that IVF requires undermines evangelicalism's witness to the integrity of God's good creation even within and under the conditions of sin. This should be reason enough to say no to *in vitro* fertilization.

Pastoral Considerations

We recognize that this is a hard word to those couples who long for children. Few desires run as deep as that one, and it can seem like a cruel burden to be denied what God seems to give so freely to other people — especially when there appear to be means available to satisfy those good desires. But as one of us has written elsewhere, our churches desperately need childless couples to help us recover the witness of lament for a tragic world, and of hope in Christ's kingdom. The gospel is good news for childless couples, who hope in Christ — not in procreation.

Pastoral counsel from within the gospel, though, requires clearheaded thinking. Those whose hearts are broken with sorrow need direction about what they may and may not pursue. We have to consider and scrutinize the extent to which the Christian moral imagination is formed more by the world's drive to overcome infertility than by a uniquely Christian response to the absence of children. As with all of God's gifts, the good desire for children can become disordered. Especially if attaining children requires a process contrary to the form of generating life that Scripture lays down as normative.

What does this argument mean for couples who have successfully conceived through IVF? Such couples *must* treat and love that child in the same way as a child conceived through marital intercourse. This child bears God's image: The wrongness of IVF is *never* imputed to the child. God loves the world so much that he gives good gifts even in and through our wrongdoing (Rom. 8:28). (This, however, is no justification for doing wrong—Rom. 6:1.)

What if a couple went through IVF and has a frozen embryo (or more) remaining? First, we'd urge them to see this embryo as a person awaiting future development: He or she is owed love, care, and respect. The embryo is also made in God's image. Second, if they have no intention to transfer him or her, we'd encourage the couple to consider allowing the embryo to be given to a family through embryo adoption. Third, we'd implore them to never allow this embryo to be destroyed or used for research. Absent these options and considering the toll that would come with possible embryo degeneration, couples might consider allowing the person they created to go into the hand of God and engage in the penitent lament that marks grief at our complicity in human death.

And if a couple is infertile and considering IVF? We'd advise them to alert their pastor and community so they do not walk through infertility alone. We'd urge them to avoid IVF, but to pursue every therapeutic medical treatment that might make natural conception more probable. Most importantly, we'd exhort them to explore how their life together might bear witness to God's kingdom by forging non-biological, parental bonds. In doing so they bear witness to a hope fundamentally fulfilled not through the birth of children, but through the advent of our Lord.

We believe, and have tried to argue, that the good news for infertile couples means saying "no" to means of generating life that are contrary to the integrity of God's good creation. We tear apart what God has joined together only at grave peril to ourselves: By dividing sex from procreation, we reconfigure the form which God has laid down for us to understand the nature of his agency in bringing new life into the world. If a people who emphasize the gospel cannot say no to that division, we are a people unworthy of our name.[xxxix]

Endnotes

i Ioannes Paulus PP. II, "Evangelium Vitae," *The Holy See*, March 25, 1995, https://www.vatican.va/content/john-paul-ii/en/encyclicals/documents/hf_jp-ii_enc_25031995_evangelium-vitae.html.

ii Selena Gomez (@selenagomez), "To see what is happening right now in Alabama, Georgia, Mississippi and several other states in our country is not only deeply upsetting but seems that it can't possibly be real," Instagram, May 18, 2019, https://www.instagram.com/p/Bxmx4CijCXC/.

iii Taylor Swift (@taylorswift13), "I'm absolutely terrified that this is where we are - that after so many decades of people fighting for women's rights to their own bodies, today's decision has stripped us of that," X, June 24, 2022, https://x.com/taylorswift13/status/1540382753677627393?lang=en.

iv "'Pro-Choice' or 'Pro-Life' Demographic Table," *Gallup*, 2024, https://news.gallup.com/poll/244709/pro-choice-pro-life-2018-demographic-tables.aspx.

v "Zero Republican Professors Found Across 33 Departments at Seven Universities: College Fix Analysis," *The College Fix*, November 29, 2022, https://www.thecollegefix.com/zero-republican-professors.

vi Voddie Baucham Jr, *Family Driven Faith: Doing What It Takes to Raise Sons and Daughters Who Walk With God* (Crossway, 2011).

vii We Need A Law, "Parental Consent for Abortion Balanced With Confidentiality," 2019, https://weneedalaw.ca/2019/02/parental-consent-for-abortion-confidentiality-and-access/.

viii Dr. Ziad Munson, *The Making of Pro-Life Activists* (University of Chicago Press, 2009).

ix Jenna Jerman, Rachel K. Jones, and Tsuyoshi Onda, 2016, "Characteristics of U.S. Abortion Patients in 2014 and

Changes Since 2008," https://www.guttmacher.org/report/characteristics-us-abortion-patients-2014.

[x] Abort73.com, 2016, "A Biblical Mandate to Do Something About Abortion," https://abort73.com/end_abortion/a_biblical_mandate_to_do_something_about_abortion/.

[xi] Elizabeth George, *A Mom After God's Own Heart: 10 Ways to Love Your Children* (Harvest House Publishers, 2005).

[xii] Justina Van Manen, *STUCK: A Complete Guide to Answering Tough Questions About Abortion* (Life Cycle Books, 2019).

[xiii] Alexander Tsiaras, "Conception to birth–visualized," TED, November 14, 2011, https://www.youtube.com/watch?v=fKyljukBE70.

[xiv] Henry Ward Beecher, *A Treasury of Illustration*, (Fleming H. Revell Company, 1904).

[xv] "The Heart of a Child," Clyde H. Box, *The Poetry of Preaching*, (Sword of the Lord Publishers, 2000).

[xvi] Taryn De Vere, "Explaining Abortion to Kids," *Medium*, May 17, 2017, https://medium.com/indian-thoughts/explaining-abortion-to-kids-4db6f15f4b76.

[xvii] Paige Alexandria, "Having the Abortion Talk With Children Is Easier Than You Think. Just Ask These Parents," *Rewire News Group*, January 13, 2020, https://rewirenewsgroup.com/2020/01/13/having-the-abortion-talk-with-children-is-easier-than-you-think-just-ask-these-parents/.

[xviii] Corrie ten Boom, *The Hiding Place* (Chosen Books, 1971).

[xix] Gregory Koukl, *Tactics: A Game Plan for Discussing Your Christian Convictions*, (Zondervan, 2019).

[xx] Ginny Kochis, "I'm Teaching Fertility Awareness to My Girls. Here's Why You Should, Too," *Not So Formulaic: Raising Exceptional Kids Rooted in Extraordinary Love*, July 26, 2017, https://notsoformulaic.com/teach-fertility-awareness-girls-why-you-should.

[xxi] Abort73.com, 2016, "A Biblical Mandate to Do Something About Abortion," https://abort73.com/end_abortion/a_biblical_mandate_to_do_something_about_abortion/.

[xxii] Bryan Kemper, "How Do You Answer Your Teenage

Daughter When She Tells You She's Pregnant?", *Life News,* January 8, 2019, https://www.lifenews.com/2019/01/08/how-do-you-answer-your-teenage-daughter-when-she-tells-you-shes-pregnant/.

[xxiii] Greta Eskridge (@maandpamodern), "Here's the thing about teens and almost teens: they are so much fun to be with! I think I love being with my kids now more than I ever have before. They make me laugh all the time. We joke together, tease each other and act silly together. They also ask great questions and have...," Instagram, (February 4, 2021), https://www.instagram.com/p/CK5Dtg_B44k/.

[xxiv] Dr. Jacqueline H. Abernathy, "I am penning an article on the cultural devaluation of the unborn," Facebook, September 11, 2016, https://www.facebook.com/jmjjch/posts/10104889844195070.

[xxv] Jenny Albers, "There Is No 'Only' in Pregnancy Loss," March 28, 2018, https://jennyalbers.com/no-pregnancy-loss/.

[xxvi] Dr. Jacqueline H. Abernathy, "One thing that compounds the grief of a miscarriage is people's heartwrenching reaction to the subsequent pregnancy," Facebook, November 11, 2016, https://www.facebook.com/jmjjch/posts/10105105161961540.

[xxvii] Stephanie Gray, "Living with LaeLae: Thoughts on My Miscarriage," *Love Unleashes Life,* November 11, 2020, https://loveunleasheslife.com/blog/2020/11/11/living-with-laelae-thoughts-on-my-miscarriage-by-stephanie-gray-connors.

[xxviii] Dr. Jacqueline H. Abernathy, "How Legal Abortion Twists Society's Response to Miscarriages," *Secular Pro-Life,* October 9, 2019, https://secularprolife.org/2019/10/how-legal-abortion-twists-societys/.

[xxix] Dr. Karen Swallow Prior, *Walking Through Infertility: Biblical, Theological, and Moral Counsel for Those Who Are Struggling,* ed. Matthew Arbo (Crossway, 2018).

[xxx] Dr. Karen Swallow Prior, "Called to Childlessness: The

Surprising Ways of God," *The Ethics and Religious Liberty Commission of the Southern Baptist Convention,* March 6, 2017, https://erlc.com/resource/called-to-childlessness-the-surprising-ways-of-god/.
xxxi Dr. Karen Swallow Prior, "Called to Childlessness: The Surprising Ways of God," *The Ethics and Religious Liberty Commission of the Southern Baptist Convention,* March 6, 2017, https://erlc.com/resource/called-to-childlessness-the-surprising-ways-of-god/.
xxxii "The Weaver," Grant Tullar, *Hope is Times of Grief,* ed. JoNancy Sundberg (Harold Shaw Publishers, 1998).
xxxiii Zacharias Ursinus, Caspar Olevianus, *The Heidelberg Catechism,* Puritan Reformed Theological Seminary, 2016, https://prts.edu/wp-content/uploads/2016/12/Heidelberg-Catechism-with-Intro.pdf.
xxxiv Jonathon Van Maren, *The Culture War* (Life Cycle Books, 2016).
xxxv Stephany Gray, "What Will Make Christians Care About Abortion?", *Love Unleashes Life,* April 23, 2018, https://loveunleasheslife.com/blog/2018/4/20/what-will-make-christians-care-about-abortion-by-stephanie-gray.
xxxvi Dr. Ziad Munson, *The Making of Pro-Life Activists* (University of Chicago Press, 2009).
xxxvii Jonathan Van Maren, host, "Episode 110: Lila Rose recounts her pro-life career," The Van Maren Show, March 25, 2021, https://thebridgehead.ca/2021/03/25/the-van-maren-show-episode-110-lila-rose-recounts-her-pro-life-career/.
xxxviii George Grant, *Third Time Around: A History of the Pro-Life Movement from the First Century to the Present* (Legacy Communications, 1991).
xxxix Matthew Lee Anderson, Andrew T. Walker, "Breaking Evangelicalism's Silence on IVF," *The Gospel Coalition,* April 25, 2019, https://www.thegospelcoalition.org/article/evangelicalisms-silence-ivf/.